MORE THAN PETTICOATS

Remarkable
FLORIDA WOMEN

MORE THAN PETTICOATS

Remarkable
FLORIDA WOMEN
Second Edition

E. Lynne Wright

Guilford, Connecticut

Copyright © 2001, 2010 Morris Book Publishing, LLC

Map: Daniel Lloyd © Morris Book Publishing, LLC

Library of Congress has cataloged the earlier edition as follows:
Wright, E. Lynne, 1931–
More than petticoats : remarkable Florida Women/E. Lynne Wright.
    p. cm.
Includes bibligraphical references and index.
ISBN 978-0-56044-933-5
 1. Women—Florida—History. 2. Women—Florida—Biography. I. Title.
HQ1438.F6 W75 2001
305.4'09759—dc21
00-51877
ISBN: 978-0-7627-5865-4
Printed in the United States of America
10 9 8 7 6 5 4 3 2 1

$14.95

CONTENTS

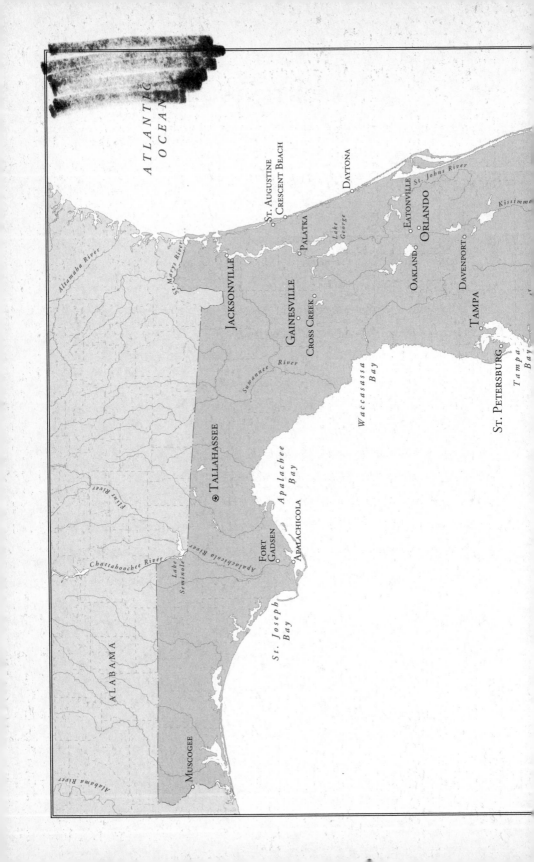

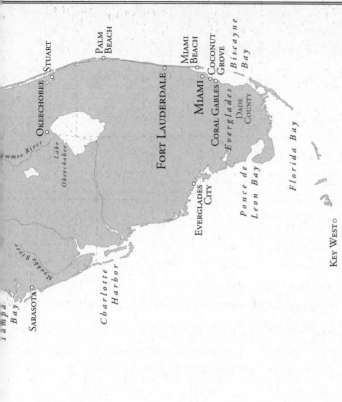

PALM
BEACH

STUART

OKEECHOBEE

MIAMI
BEACH

COCONUT
GROVE

FORT LAUDERDALE

MIAMI

CORAL GABLES

*Biscayne
Bay*

Everglades

DADE
COUNTY

*Ponce de
Leon Bay*

*Biscayne
Bay*

EVERGLADES
CITY

Florida Bay

*Lake
Okeechobee*

Kissimmee River

Myakka River

*Charlotte
Harbor*

SARASOTA

*Tampa
Bay*

KEY WEST

GULF OF
MEXICO

0   50   100 kilometers

0   50   100 miles

ACKNOWLEDGMENTS

Among the many Florida libraries and archives that have generously provided me with information are: the Miami-Dade Main Public Library, the Jacksonville Main Library, the Tampa-Hillsborough Public Library, the Tebeau-Field Library of Florida History, the Schlesinger Library at Radcliffe, and the Indian River County Main Library, my second home. I thank them all. I am indebted to Peg Wilson, in Vero Beach, who secured countless interlibrary loans for me. Thanks, too, to Ginger Young, former registrar at the Sanford L. Ziff Jewish Museum of Florida in Miami Beach; Marilyn Rathbun, research director at the Fort Lauderdale Historical Society; Professor Nancy Hewitt at Rutgers University; Judy Hoanshelt, former liaison for Miami Beach to the Florida Commission on the Status of Women; the University of North Florida at Jacksonville for access to the Eartha M. M. White Collection; the Miami Beach Chamber of Commerce; the Elliot Museum; the Jensen Beach Chamber of Commerce; and the Florida Oceanographic Coastal Center. I am grateful to the Florida State Archives at Tallahassee for photo permissions; and to Dr. Lewis Wynne, former director of the Florida Historical Society, and Debra Wynne, archivist at the Florida Historical Society for their help. I thank my editors Charlene Patterson and Meredith Davis Rufino, both wise and endlessly patient. Last, I thank my family for their encouragement and support, especially my husband, Dr. George Wright, who is always "on call" for me.

INTRODUCTION

Women's history, ignored for so long that many people thought there was none, is, after all, half the human experience, lived by the half that does two-thirds of the work, receives one-tenth of the earnings, owns less than 1 percent of world property, and comprises 16.8 percent of the 111th Congress.

Our Founding Mothers were primarily immigrants who faced a life of unending, backbreaking labor to provide food, shelter, doctoring, education, and clothing for their families. Not uncommonly, they also gave birth every year, a health-depleting hardship.

They also found time to serve their country. Along with boycotting British tea during the Revolution, women donned men's clothing, armed themselves with muskets and pitchforks, and defended bridges at Lexington and Concord, capturing retreating British soldiers.

Lucretia Mott and Elizabeth Cady Stanton fought tirelessly against slavery; then, denied seats at antislavery conventions due to their gender, they organized a women's rights convention and recycled the Founding Fathers' words into the central document of women's history. They and Susan B. Anthony were memorialized in a statue commissioned in 1921; the statue languished in the basement of the U.S. Capitol until 1997, when it was finally moved upstairs.

Even though most were denied the education their brothers were privileged to receive, the women of the 1800s produced *Uncle Tom's Cabin*, the "Battle Hymn of the Republic," and the words engraved on the Statue of Liberty, when they weren't striving to secure their rights.

The industrialization of America led women to factory jobs, long hours, poor pay, and dangerous working conditions. Women's clubs proliferated and soon had millions of members working for reforms but gaining little advancement for themselves.

In 1920 the Nineteenth Amendment was passed, leading to more active participation in public life, though many doors remained closed until the war years of the 1940s, when six million women were employed. Five years later, the men returned from the war, and, after keeping war production lines moving, ferrying planes overseas, and ducking bullets to tend the wounded, women were told the work was too hard for them and they were relieved of their jobs.

The 1950s produced particularly scurrilous propaganda against working women. Female ambition, described as mental illness that caused alcoholic husbands and homosexual children, nevertheless endured in the person of women doctors, scientists, writers, artists, and others subjected to incredible pressures.

Florida women have their share of heroes. Although unacknowledged and disenfranchised, these women worked to improve life against existing culture under sometimes dangerous, sometimes humiliating conditions. On the Florida frontier, Spanish, European, African, and Native American cultures clashed, and poisonous snakes, lightning strikes, hurricanes, mosquitoes, and alligators abounded. Through it all, these women, clad in corsets and long skirts through intense summer heat, made homes, established public libraries and hospitals, and worked for education, conservation, public health, and minority rights.

Mary McLeod Bethune, daughter of slaves, founded Bethune-Cookman College in Daytona. Miami is the only major American city that owes its existence to a woman—Julia Tuttle. Our unique Everglades would already be just another cookie-cutter housing development were it not for Marjory Stoneman Douglas. Zora Neale Hurston, a black writer who died penniless in Fort Pierce, is now studied in colleges and compared to Faulkner. Fifteen-year-old Seminole Malee Francis had the courage to stand up to the prevailing power structure, which happened to be Native American, in defense of a human life, which happened to be white.

There are more, hundreds of them, in Florida and beyond, famous and anonymous. I hope this book will help to bring at least a few of the remarkable Florida women out of the shadows, into public consciousness and perhaps the history books, where they belong. We thank them for allowing us to stand on their shoulders.

MALEE FRANCIS

FLORIDA'S POCAHONTAS

It was on or about August 27, 1818, and the still Florida air almost dripped its humidity. A group of 188 bedraggled Indians, mostly women and children in starving condition, shuffled silently into Fort Gadsden near the mouth of the Apalachicola River on Florida's Gulf Coast. They surrendered themselves to the fort's commander, Colonel Matthew Arbuckle. Among them were the recent widow and two daughters of the Prophet Francis. The younger daughter, fifteen-year-old Malee, or Milly, as she was known to the Americans, was strikingly beautiful and was well known to the whites for having saved the life of one of their soldiers.

Nearly overwhelmed by their numbers and their sorry condition, Colonel Arbuckle did all in his power to tend to their immediate needs, providing food, water, medicines, and a place for them to rest. He also sent word to the soldier Malee had saved, Private Duncan McKrimmon, who had been returned to his home in Milledgeville, Georgia.

While Malee and the group rested, regaining their strength, the young soldier made his way to Fort Gadsden, carrying donations from Milledgeville citizens, who were eager to show their appreciation for Malee's efforts on McKrimmon's behalf. Remembering how she had interceded for him at the risk of her own life, Private McKrimmon presented her with the gifts and asked her to be his wife.

Malee gratefully accepted the donations, which she shared with the other Indians, but she gracefully declined his offer of matrimony. "I did not save you for that," she said. "I do not want any man." Colonel Arbuckle reported that Malee said she saved McKrimmon's life "from feelings of humanity alone, and that she would have rendered the same service to any other white man similarly circumstanced." She was therefore "not disposed to accept of his offer of matrimony."

The nobility of her sentiments is extraordinary when one considers that already in her young life she had been witness to countless perfidious acts by white invaders and untold numbers of cruelties on both sides. Perhaps the beautiful fifteen-year-old girl had decided, "Enough." If so, Private Duncan McKrimmon was the beneficiary of her mature decision.

Malee was born about 1803, the youngest daughter of Hillis Hadjo, known in English as the Prophet Francis or Josiah Francis, a prominent Creek chief who was the offspring of an Englishman and a Creek woman. Malee's older sister's name is unrecorded, and there was also a boy named Earle, about whom some mystery persists. Earle was said to have become a silversmith and a prophet like his father, and like his father, he died at the hands of whites, but in a Montgomery jail.

Malee's mother was the only family member who did not speak any English. Since most Indian girls received little education except from their mothers, Francis must have taken it upon himself to instruct his children in English, at least.

Confusion abounded among whites with regard to Indian names. Girls usually kept the same name they were given at birth, but not so with boys. At birth a boy was given his baby name, such as "Little Cub," then another name when he reached warrior age and completed a dangerous deed, and sometimes a third one later, after he completed another daring act. Further, as males achieved other goals, still more names were added. *Hillis hayas* were medicine men; whites frequently called them prophets. Warriors often had second names—Hadjo, Francis's name, meant "furious battle." Whites muddled things even further by phonetically writing Indian names, which they heard through ears accustomed to white names, such as Milly for Malee.

In the early 1800s, Spain, Britain, and America battled each other and the Indians for control of Florida, rendering it a scene of never-ending maneuverings. With the outbreak of the War of 1812, Francis, who then lived with his family near the Chattahoochee River in what is now Alabama, was enlisted by a friend to join the English cause. He was known to have assisted the British against Andrew Jackson and the Americans. When Jackson initiated his brutal raids against the Creeks in 1813 and 1814, Francis took his family south, establishing a new Seminole village in Spanish Florida, south of Tallahassee, near Fort St. Marks.

In 1816 Francis, accompanied by a British officer, embarked on a trip to England where, in recognition of his assistance, he was received with great ceremony by Prince Regent George IV. He was commissioned a brigadier general in the British army, presented with a diamond snuff box, an elaborate uniform of red and gold, 325 British pounds, and a tomahawk mounted in gold. An elegant ball was held in his honor aboard a Russian frigate anchored nearby, where trumpets heralded his arrival, according to London newspapers. But interestingly, Francis never tried to help England after that. He sailed home, determined to live at peace with the white man.

Upon her father's return from England in June 1817, Malee received many presents of "dresses, shoes and bonnets and much unaccustomed finery and learned to make graceful use of them."

At that time, hostilities were escalating among the Americans, the Spaniards, the British, and the Indians, resulting in another invasion by Andrew Jackson's army in early 1818. Entering Florida near the mouth of the Chattahoochee River, Jackson continued along the Apalachicola River to a defunct fort, where he built another garrison, naming it Fort Gadsden.

While his army was at rest, Private Duncan McKrimmon, Second Regiment of the Georgia militia attached to General Jackson's army, went fishing early one morning, became confused trying to return to camp, and was lost for several days. He was wandering about, trying to find his way, when he was spotted by a party of unfriendly Indians who overpowered him and took him to the town of the Prophet Francis.

Francis, appearing in his splendid uniform with a brace of pistols on his belt, proudly displayed his British commission to the prisoner. He then allowed the captors to interrogate McKrimmon, who eventually gave them the information they wanted regarding the strength and location of the American forces. That done, they prepared him for sacrifice.

McKrimmon was stripped naked and his face was blackened with soot before he was tied to a stake. Bone-chilling war cries commenced, magnifying the young man's terror.

Malee and her sister, who were playing on the riverbank near their home, immediately understood the significance of what they heard and hurried in the direction of the sounds. Seeing the terrified youth who was not much older than they were, they stopped. He was tied to a tree and helpless while two warriors danced menacingly around him with rifles ready to shoot, and onlookers stood by with approving expressions on their faces. Malee, overcome with sadness, remained silent, unable to participate in the merriment surrounding her.

It was their right, she knew, for it was accepted that if an Indian caught a white person, he had that life in his power and could not be interfered with, not even by a chief. Seeing the terror on the young prisoner's face, Malee ran to her father, imploring him to do something, but, as she knew he would, he said he was helpless, that she should speak to the captors. It was her only chance to affect the outcome.

Racing back to the warriors, she begged them to stop, saying Mc-Krimmon was just a boy. One of the warriors became enraged, telling her he had lost two sisters in the war with the white men. Unwilling to give up, Malee kept on pleading, reminding him that killing the prisoner wouldn't bring his sisters back. The warriors were unmoved.

When it seemed all was lost, when the captors were ready "to terminate forever the mortal existence of the unfortunate McKrimmon," as reported by the *Georgia Journal,* Malee placed herself between the captive and death, telling the "astonished executioner, if he thirsted for blood, to shed hers."

Challenged by the brave daughter of their chief, the two warriors finally relented. They agreed to let McKrimmon live if he would consent to have his head shaved and not try to escape.

Without hesitation, McKrimmon agreed. His head was shaved, except for a scalp lock, which the Indians adorned with feathers. After they painted him and dressed him in their style, they considered him adopted.

Malee showed McKrimmon much kindness for the next several days, before he was taken away to Fort St. Marks, where his ransom was negotiated with a sympathetic Spanish commander named Luengo. He was released for seven and a half gallons of rum and permitted to rejoin his army.

Preceding Jackson's army into Fort St. Marks in April were two schooners sent there to act as reinforcements. They made their way up the Appalachee River, where they anchored, flying British flags to conceal their identity. The newly freed McKrimmon, having been informed of the schooners' mission, rowed out and boarded one ship, the *Thomas Shields.* Since British flags were displayed, Francis and another chief rowed out to visit what they thought was a friendly ship. The captain welcomed them onboard, inviting them to his cabin for refreshments. As they followed him, several Americans emerged from hiding, rushed toward the two Indians, and captured them. Inside the ship, American flags were prominently exhibited.

When McKrimmon appeared, Francis scornfully reminded him of how his life had been spared such a short time before.

"You did not save my life," the private replied. "It was your daughter. I will do all I can to save you."

That afternoon, Malee was seen paddling around the schooner, apparently searching for her father. Suddenly, shots were fired on her from the ship. She grabbed a rifle she had concealed in the bottom of her canoe and returned fire before disappearing.

McKrimmon's efforts at saving the lives of the two chiefs were fruitless when Andrew Jackson arrived the next morning and received a report on the previous day's events. Jackson had previously written to Washington, "The Prophet Francis . . . is exciting the Seminoles to hostility. . . . It is important that these men should be captured and made an example of." Now, Francis was in Jackson's power and, still clad in his opulent British uniform, was hanged along with his friend.

Within days, Jackson ordered the execution of two more men—British traders engaged in legitimate trade, but of whom Jackson was suspicious. One of them, a man named Armbrister, was much smitten with Malee and had proposed marriage to her, but she declined. It was said by some that after Armbrister's death, Malee could be found lying "upon his grave every moon, weeping."

After Francis's death, conditions in his village continued to decline, and shortly after the mass surrender at Fort Gadsden, his family joined other Seminoles on the long, difficult journey to Oklahoma Territory for resettlement.

Years passed, during which there is no recorded account of Malee's exact whereabouts or activities. We only know that she survived the journey of hundreds of miles from her familiar, verdant home to a strange, new country.

On their way to and in the Oklahoma Territory, Malee's tribe had to compete with other tribes for scarce resources. Indian agents and contractors hired by the government to guarantee provisions for the migrating tribes along the way and for one year after they were resettled, grafted supplies, depriving the Indians. In 1842, under intense political pressure, President John Tyler chose Colonel Ethan Allen Hitchcock, grandson of Ethan Allen, the Revolutionary War legend, to conduct an inquiry into the activities of Indian agents.

Hitchcock was a man of unimpeachable honor and unassailable credentials. While on his mission, he heard about Malee's saving of Mc-Krimmon's life and that she was living nearby, near the Arkansas River, close to where the present-day town of Muskogee, Oklahoma, is located. Hitchcock sent for her and when she arrived, he saw that, after a difficult life, she was "still attractive." She verified the facts of the story as he had heard them, adding that following relocation, she had married an Indian man who had since died. Although she had had eight children, just three were living, two boys and a girl. Times were very hard, she said, and she and her children lived in poverty.

When Hitchcock returned to Washington, he made no attempt to soften his opinion of Jackson's conduct in Florida, nor did his damaging report spare others. Because of it, reforms were instituted and he immediately set out to procure a small government pension for Malee. After delaying considerably, Congress passed a bill to provide Malee with ninety-six dollars a year for the rest of her life "as a testimonial of the gratitude and bounty of the United States, for the humanity displayed by her." Further, it was enacted that a "medal with appropriate devices impressed thereon" be given to her as an additional testimonial of the gratitude of the United States.

Congress passed the bill two years later, and then took another three years before getting the proclamation to Malee. By the time Indian agent James Logan reached her with the news, she was very ill with tuberculosis and "in dying circumstances." Agent Logan reported to his superiors in June 1848 that he immediately procured medical aid for her and "did all that was possible to alleviate her sufferings" while reading the proclamation to her. "She was so highly elated," he wrote, "that I flattered myself she was recovering."

She did not recover. Florida's Pocahontas died on May 19, 1848, and was buried somewhere between the city of Muskogee and the banks of the Arkansas River.

Malee did not live long enough to receive a cent of her pension or her medal, the only one in United States history ever specially awarded to a woman.

BERTHA HONORÉ PALMER

1849–1918

DIAMONDS AND CATTLE RANCHES

I t was January 1910 and the temperature outside would never get much colder. Trying to ignore the penetrating, frigid wind that blew down the 307 miles of icy Lake Michigan and then battered the snow-crusted windows of her Chicago mansion took all the concentration Mrs. Potter Palmer could muster. Stoically, she continued reading the classified ads in the *Sunday Chicago Tribune,* since shifting real estate values always interested her. One ad in particular caught her eye. It eloquently described the beauty of Sarasota Bay on Florida's west coast, naming J. H. Lord as the realtor to contact for details concerning some of the "richest land in the world" for sale at a pittance. The timing could not have been better. Imagining palm trees swaying under warm, sunny, blue skies, the wealthy widow asked her father, H. H. Honoré, to look into it for her. He did and within days J. H. Lord was visiting the Palmer mansion, securing a promise from Chicago's uncrowned queen to visit the Sarasota area the following month.

Bertha Honoré Palmer, widowed for eight years, felt ready for a new challenge, a shift in her way of life. At age sixty-one, she had reached a place in life where being the self-described "nation's hostess and head woman servant" was losing its luster. An international figure who was a friend of royalty, who entertained statesmen, who was a confidante of celebrities, and who was a pacesetter for party-givers, she was increasingly uncomfortable with her one-sided reputation.

One publication wrote that "people are concerned not so much about what she thinks as they are about her aloof manner, her stunning carriage, the smooth pink and white unwrinkled skin, the perfect teeth, wonderful

Bertha Honoré Palmer   Library of Congress, Z62-107005

hair, velvet gowns, her world famous furs and the sumptuous way in which she conducts her ménage." Why, she wondered, did they see only that when she was so much more? Why did they ignore her speeches against the forced dependence and helplessness of women? Why was it never mentioned when she held meetings with factory girls in her home to study their working and living conditions in order to push for protective legislation? All anyone ever seemed to see were her parties and her diamonds.

She was not tired of her life. She enjoyed it to the fullest, but the promise of a simpler existence in a small town for at least part of the year held enormous appeal.

Bertha Mathilde Honoré was born into a distinguished southern family in Louisville, Kentucky, on May 22, 1849. When she was six, her father, Henry Hamilton Honoré, moved the family to Chicago, where he opened a shop selling cutlery and imported hardware. Chicago's population was already eighty thousand and growing. Bertha's father made substantial investments in real estate while her mother, Eliza, attracted a social clique. Bertha, with her brothers, Adrian, Henry, Nathaniel, and Lockwood, and her sister, Ida, lived in style in their spacious home, among congenial neighbors.

Mingling with the prospering people in Mr. Honoré's circle was Potter Palmer, a young man originally from New York. Potter reshaped the way department stores did business by introducing the practices of giving credit and exchanging merchandise that proved unsatisfactory. He was responsible for adding dash to women's shopping experiences. He drilled his clerks on presenting goods with a flourish and maintaining courtesy at all times.

As business contacts between Bertha's father and Palmer became more frequent, so, too, did Palmer's visits to the Honoré home. Many years in the future, Potter would tell his son that when he first saw thirteen-year-old Bertha during one of those visits, he made up his mind he would wait for her to grow up, and then he would marry her.

Bertha, meanwhile, excelled in her studies, including chemistry, ancient and modern geography, logic and intellectual philosophy, astronomy and botany, meteorology, rhetoric, literature, composition, algebra, geometry, and domestic economy. She took honors in piano, vocal, and harp music and, after graduation, made her debut at the splendid new Honoré home on Michigan Avenue.

While Bertha was growing up, Potter was amassing a fortune. Successful in merchandising, he invested brilliantly, and by age forty-four, he had turned the five-thousand-dollar stake from his father into more than 7 million dollars. He was heavily involved in civic endeavors while overseeing the completion of the fabulous new 3.5-million-dollar Palmer House hotel, his wedding gift to his new bride. They were the first to occupy the bridal suite in August 1870.

The wedding ceremony took place in the Honoré home, and shortly after, the couple embarked on an ocean voyage to Europe, Bertha's first ever. She returned home with new clothes and jewels, art objects, and an adoring husband. There was no reason to think life would ever be less.

But a short fourteen months later, while Potter was out of town attending a funeral, the fire blamed on Mrs. O'Leary's cow roared through the city, destroying the properties of the Honoré and Palmer families, along with many others. The news traveled to Potter in upstate New York, and, after being reassured of his wife's safety, he sent a message instructing her to help others in any way she could. His instructions were unnecessary as his bride had already taken in as many refugees as could fit into their home and begun efforts to feed and clothe the many made homeless by the calamity. By the time the inferno had burned itself out, three hundred people were dead, ninety thousand were homeless, and seventeen thousand buildings were gone, along with one-third of Chicago's wealth.

After an initial period of discouragement, Chicagoans rose to the challenge, and with help arriving from all over the country, and even the world, soon, larger and better buildings replaced the charred ones. Potter Palmer and Henry Honoré led the way in the rebirth of the city.

The Palmers had barely recovered from that disaster when the financial panic of 1873 dealt them another severe financial blow. In 1874 the young couple became parents for the first time when son Honoré was born. A few months later, Bertha's sister married Frederick Dent Grant, son of Ulysses S. Grant, at the Honoré home, drawing national attention, and from that summer on, trouble seemed to reside elsewhere. The Palmers' second son, Potter, was born in 1875, completing the family.

The Palmers had their own quarters in the Palmer House, which had gained a worldwide reputation for magnificence, attracting royalty, presidents, gold rush millionaires, Edwin Booth, Buffalo Bill, Sarah Bernhardt, Rudyard Kipling, and Jenny Lind. Although Potter worked long hours at the hotel and Bertha was devoted to raising her sons, they each managed to find time for civic endeavors, Potter with the YMCA and the Civic League and Bertha with the WCTU and Jane Addams's Hull House. She consistently gave her money and time toward efforts for better education for women and equal pay for equal work. At the same time, she had no patience with some of what she considered the cruder strategies of the Bloomer girls and suffragettes. Placing emphasis on women's inborn assets seemed to her the better approach.

In 1891 Bertha was named chairman of the Board of Lady Managers for the World's Columbian Exposition to be held in Chicago in 1893. The Palmers traveled to Europe, where Bertha's personal friendship with politicians and rulers who had been hotel guests helped in obtaining exhibits from forty-seven countries for the Woman's Building, where women's achievements and the barriers they still faced were demonstrated. The task was enormous, but Bertha threw all her energies into it, cementing old ties to world leaders and forging new ones along with, inevitably, making some enemies. Even some women were opposed to women "flaunting their powers outside the home." Others were unwilling to share their self-importance or allow others to bask in their hard-earned sunshine. The Woman's Building itself was Bertha's crowning achievement, designed by a woman and filled with the work of women painters and sculptors, including a mural by Mary Cassatt. Bertha concluded her speech at the dedication ceremonies by announcing, "Even more important than the discovery of Columbus, which we are gathered together to celebrate, is the fact that the General Government has just discovered woman."

In a letter, the governor of Illinois praised her work, stating, "The cause of women's independence has been advanced a century through the Columbian Exposition."

The Palmers tolerated a brief period of enforced idleness during which Bertha recharged her energies and Potter rested from ever increasing bouts of disabling rheumatism. He had white hair and beard by now, and the difference in their ages was noticeable, but they were content with each other and with their lives. His pride in her was obvious. At one glittering social occasion, he stood to the side with a friend, watching her. "There she stands with $200,000 worth of jewels on her," he said in obvious pride.

In 1900 President McKinley appointed Bertha the only female member of the national commission representing the United States at the Paris Exposition. She fulfilled her role with her usual efficient flair. After the exposition closed, she was awarded the Legion of Honor for her work.

In 1902 Potter's frail health worsened. After being ill with grippe, he developed edema of the lungs and died unexpectedly, with his wife and sons attending him. He willed his entire fortune to Bertha, without any strings. Having been reminded by his attorney that she could conceivably marry again after his death, generous Potter had replied, "If she does, he'll need the money," and the will stood.

Bertha lived quietly during her mourning period and then gradually resumed normal activity, always with the support of her sons and the rest of her family. There were more European visits and stays at Newport and Bar Harbor as a restlessness built inside her until the *Chicago Tribune* ad for Florida real estate appeared. After that, a new life opened to her.

On February 10, 1910, Bertha, accompanied by her father, her two sons, and her brother Adrian, arrived in Sarasota, a fishing village of nine hundred people, where they were met by A. B. Edwards, partner of the realtor J. H. Lord. Edwards, having been alerted by Lord as to her arrival, prevailed upon the owner of a newly finished sanitarium to permit its use as a temporary hotel for the "queen of Chicago," since the only hotel in the area was so rundown, he feared it might send a society woman running off. The sanitarium was always spotless, and with some further sprucing up and some pieces of new furniture, it would do nicely.

The Floridians were as pleasantly surprised by the down-to-earth quality of Bertha and her party as she was impressed with Sarasota. A sightseeing voyage on the sparkling waters of Little Sarasota Bay was all the convincing Bertha needed, and soon she owned eighty thousand acres of Florida real estate. "Here is heaven, at last," she told her father, envisioning the best of all the European resorts she had visited.

With her usual zest, she set about buying more land, hiring experts to help with the planning, and making the necessary contacts to bring in improvements, beginning with a railroad spur and roads. She hired an architect to design her home, to be called The Oaks, and, never one to enter projects blindly, brought in geologists, gardeners, engineers, and other experts to teach her what she needed to know. She studied, listened to advice, and then made decisions, some right, some wrong. She brought more people to the area when she hired workers to clear trees, build seawalls, tend her thirteen-hundred-acre grove, and pack and ship her grapefruit to Chicago. It was the Potter Palmer method of doing business: invest and do good. A shortage of laborers required her to import even more people from the outside—blacks, Italians, and others—fostering irritation among the native workers, who would have caused even more trouble had it not been for the fact that Bertha paid the highest wages around and had already earned a reputation for fairness. Then, too, it was undeniable that she was the spark for Sarasota's boom times, to the benefit of many.

It seemed no time at all before she was shipping her grapefruit back to the Midwest and her celery crop was thriving.

Bertha's next challenge was to launch a cattle ranch in the Myakka River region. Touring with Edwards by horse and carriage, she was so taken with the area that upon being told six thousand acres were for sale, she authorized him to buy it for her. "Much as if she were ordering a bag of peanuts," he said. When the seller said he must first sell the cattle on his land, she bought his cattle, too, and named her acquisition Meadow Sweet Pastures.

Among her mistakes on the ranch was building silos for storing grain, customary among cattlemen in the Midwest but unnecessary in Florida since cattle could graze year round. Native ranchers laughed, then laughed again when she imported seventeen prize Brahma bulls to crossbreed with her cattle. She built vats to dip her herd for ticks, causing much derision since the prevailing belief of the time was that ticks came from within the animal. When her herd's ticks were wiped out and her herd became so prized she was the first ever to ship a trainload of cattle out of state—and to Texas, of all places—the laughing stopped.

Although she had tried to placate local ranchers, giving barbecues, visiting their wives, and always being cautious about showing respect for their pride, she went against the tradition of free-range ranching when she fenced in some of her acreage as a protective measure for her cattle. It was a move that provoked the prickly locals to cut her fences under cover of night, and, without fail, anytime she left town, her property and workers were attacked. After one such raid, when her sleeping black workers were shot at, she sent a warning to the locals' hangout, saying, "I have been greatly annoyed by the annual criminal assaults on my place and on my innocent, sleeping Negroes, by cowardly bands of armed men who came at night to shoot them up and drive them away. Every investor wants to know first of all about labor conditions, and to find a community away back in the atrocities of the lawless Ku Klux era finishes its case at once."

With her long winter stays in Florida and her travels to London, Paris, and New York, she spent less and less time in Chicago, but Bertha kept up contacts and lifelong friendships there. She maintained an avid interest in art, donating a number of impressionist paintings to the Chicago Art Institute and providing a gold medal with a thousand-dollar prize for the most promising young artist one year.

Wherever she went, she kept a close watch on every detail of her holdings in Florida, sending minute instructions to her overseer and closely monitoring expenses. She once sent him a sketch detailing exactly how the vines were to be trained on poles for her garden.

The outbreak of World War I sent her scurrying from Paris home to The Oaks where she entertained all three of her grandchildren, providing them with ponies and riding lessons, books, toolboxes, and pets.

She traveled to Palm Beach for a wartime benefit ball that included a competition for the title of Queen of Jewels. One woman wore a seven-and-a-half-foot-long chain of matched diamonds and a string of pearls that had belonged to Marie Antoinette. Another entry had a necklace worth half a million dollars. Bertha's jewels were worth less monetarily but combined with her demeanor and carriage, were deemed worthy of the royal title.

The arrival of Mrs. Potter Palmer in Sarasota was a catalyst for change in the slumbering little town. Publicity in northern newspapers about her and about the Ringling Brothers, the circus family who arrived a year later, helped lure others to the area. Besides managing her own spread, Bertha involved herself in civic affairs, helping establish a women's club by donating land and two thousand dollars to get it started. As with other women's groups of the era, the club was instrumental in starting a library, building parks, and instigating other beautification projects.

For Christmas in 1916, the Honoré family gathered in Chicago to honor Bertha's father, who, at ninety-three, was still hearty enough to attend to business at his office every day. Shortly after the celebration, his health failed and he died. Bertha had come to rely on his good advice after Potter's death, and she very much missed the old man. Her own robust health began a steady decline.

She told no one but her immediate family when she was diagnosed with breast cancer. Even after she underwent a mastectomy, few were aware of it as she continued most of her activities without complaint. Giving final orders to her ranch manager, she said, "I will never go back to the ranch. I have gone there for the last time." With her sons at her side, she died on May 5, 1918.

The mayor personally lowered the city flag as Sarasota grieved. The woman whose entry into town was greeted with glee by real estate dealers, with awe by average citizens, and with derision by cattle ranchers, left behind a Palmer First National Bank and Trust Company, Palmer Ranch, Palmer Garden Center, Palmer Florida Corporation, and five streets with family names within the city. She more than doubled the eight-million-dollar estate her husband left at his death.

Shortly before she died, one magazine wrote of her rare gift for diplomacy: "When men have it they are called diplomats; when women have it they are called tactful. Occasionally there is a woman who possesses it in such superlative degree and quality that she is admitted to the rank of diplomats. All who know her admit grudgingly that Bertha Honoré Palmer is a diplomat."

Her obvious enjoyment of her wealth was redeemed by the generous gifts she bestowed where they would do the most good. Mrs. Potter Palmer traveled the world and made a journey from society pages to the history books.

JULIA TUTTLE

1849–1898
MOTHER OF MIAMI

The young society matron clasped the hands of her children, Fannie and Harry, as she stepped off the mail boat, seeing for the first time the tiny Florida settlement where her father had been homesteading a tract of land. Back home in Cleveland, people compared Miami to the Wild West, erroneously, since the railroads had already reached as far west as Wyoming, but it had taken Julia Tuttle several railroads, a riverboat, a cattle cart, a schooner, and a barge to reach her father's home. Upon arriving, she found nothing but a deserted army camp, the old Fort Dallas, plus several plantations and an Indian trading post. Still, like her father, Julia saw something else, something no one else seemed to see.

Julia's father, Ephraim Sturtevant, a teacher turned businessman, was sixty-seven years old when he and his third wife, Frances, fifty-seven years old and also a teacher, joined their neighbors, the Brickells, in moving to the wilderness. Julia, who remained at home with her adult siblings, remembered the Cleveland neighbors' guffaws as they swapped stories about her parents and their friends searching for the Fountain of Youth.

Even after some northern newspapers had begun taking an interest in the Florida peninsula, there were detractors. One writer commenting on conditions in Florida in the late 1800s said,

> The scale of living was pretty low. People lived on potatoes and other easily grown vegetables, fish, birds and once in a while would have some venison when somebody would shoot a deer. It was inordinately difficult to obtain groceries, such as flour, coffee, sugar and canned goods, and anyway, most people couldn't

Julia Tuttle   Florida State Archives

afford to buy them most of the time. Travel and communication were both difficult and dangerous, there being rivers with swift currents, wild animals, snakes and roaming beach tramps with criminal tendencies to tend with.

Julia, however, thrilled at the sight of the mangrove-lined Miami River flowing into the jewel-like brilliant turquoise of Biscayne Bay. She understood her parents' fascination with the tropical scene before her.

Julia Deforest Sturtevant was born in Cleveland, Ohio, on January

22, 1849, where, after completing her education in languages, music, and botany, she celebrated her eighteenth birthday by marrying handsome, dashing Frederick Leonard Tuttle, who was employed in his family's iron ore business. Frederick's father, Henry B. Tuttle, was the man who gave John D. Rockefeller his first job, a connection that would later prove to be an asset to Julia.

With no financial worries, the young couple moved into a fashionable home they named Gaydene. They enjoyed a privileged life that included raising orchids and teaching Sunday school at the Euclid Baptist Church where they and John D. Rockefeller were members.

Julia became a mother at nineteen when Frances Emmalie, or Fannie, was born. Almost from the start, vivacious Fannie seemed to delight in testing her mother, a habit that persisted all her life. Baby brother Henry Ethelbert, called Harry by the family, arrived on the scene two years later and soon contracted an illness that resulted in an atrophied arm. Understandably, Julia was a typical anguished mother who for five years journeyed periodically with her son to Philadelphia hospitals for treatments that produced few results other than distancing her more and more from her daughter. Family members agreed Julia pampered the boy far too much, further contributing to Fannie's pique. In time, Julia detached herself enough from Harry to send him to boarding school in Connecticut.

Before his departure, Julia took her children and a friend, a Mrs. Davis, with her to visit her parents in Florida. By then, the Sturtevants were well established on the peninsula, Ephraim serving as county judge and later as a state senator.

At that time, for a woman to travel such a distance unescorted was scandalous. For Julia, it made sense. Her husband was unable to get away, and she wanted her children to have the experience of visiting their grandparents in the balmy wilderness.

When the two lone women and the children stepped ashore, it caused a minor sensation among the locals. Later in the visit, Julia toured the area, unchaperoned, in a sailboat with a gentleman named J. W. Ewan, causing tongues to wag even more.

Ewan, known as the Duke of Dade, formerly of Charleston, South Carolina, was a charming man who at various times was engaged as postmaster, county treasurer, and state legislator. He was said to be entranced with Julia, even though she was a married woman with two children in tow and had nothing more on her mind than learning as much as she could about the untamed beauty of her surroundings. One friend of the Duke's, George Parsons, described Julia as "full of life but not very discreet," given, he said, to "rather unbecoming conduct in a married lady." He further stated,

> *Mrs. Tuttle very goodlooking & lively . . . Ewan and I took the ladies around showing them the place and all objects of interest and after supper, which was a woeful one, we visited some Indians who were camped for the night near Brickell's and the ladies were quite interested, though somewhat alarmed as the Indians were not very sober and I had to take hold of one young buck to prevent him from embracing Mrs. Davis.*

Julia returned to Cleveland either unaware or unconcerned about such opinions.

When Frederick developed tuberculosis, a disease common in those days, he was forced to retire early from the iron ore business. He coped with his long illness by writing unremarkable poetry, painting on china, and reading.

Along with her charity work and volunteer chores at the Euclid Baptist Church, Julia, with some trepidation, visited Frederick's iron works, tentatively making some business judgments, a novelty for her as it was for most other women at the time. To her surprise, she found she enjoyed the work, finding satisfaction in making decisions and completing deals.

As her husband's health deteriorated, Julia decided to take him to visit her parents, hoping the climate would help him regain some strength. It did for a time, but in 1886, four years after the death of her father, Frederick died, leaving her feeling very much alone and the sole provider for her children.

It took Julia the better part of a year to settle Frederick's estate and when she finished, she learned she was left with only a few thousand dollars and their Cleveland home. Fatigued, dispirited, and frightened that her children might have inherited a weakened constitution from their father, she asked J. D. Rockefeller to try to persuade his friend Henry Flagler to hire her as a housekeeper for his new hotel in St. Augustine. Flagler's rather brusque answer was "No." Since there was no one else to rely on, she recognized she would have to make some important decisions. A trip to England and another to California convinced her that Florida was where she and her children belonged. With assistance from the Duke of Dade, she purchased abandoned Fort Dallas and 640 acres of land on the north side of the Miami River.

In 1891, accompanied by her now adult children, her housekeeper Maggie Carney, two Jersey cows, and many prized possessions from Gaydene, including paintings, china, and goblets, Julia arrived to begin her new life in Florida. The date was November 13, and to Fannie's great annoyance, superstitious Julia would not permit anyone to disembark until the following dawn.

While the cows were dispatched to the fort barracks, Julia moved her party into the deserted officers' quarters where she unpacked her china and crystal and then set about clearing the surrounding jungle and remodeling the two-story building into a comfortable home, complete with a windmill, wharf, boathouse, and stables. She hired divers to secure some splendid tile from a shipwreck off the Florida reef, which she used for flooring.

In adopting the ways of her pioneering neighbors, Julia learned that reaping the rewards of nearby shipwrecks was cause for celebration.

Providing no lives were lost, and that seldom happened, the wrecks were much appreciated diversions, since divers salvaged household furniture, canned goods, ready-made clothing, and even baby carriages, all items hard to come by.

Influenced by the stories told by her mother, who at one time had taught Seminole Indians in Tallahassee, Julia befriended her Seminole neighbors. One in particular, a chief named Matlo, became her great friend, visiting weekly with gifts of venison and bear meat. It was rumored that Matlo and the Duke of Dade were both interested in marrying Julia, but she allowed nothing to interfere with her vision.

She wrote to a friend, "It may seem strange to you but it is the dream of my life to see this wilderness turned into a prosperous country and where this tangled mass of vine brush, trees and rocks now are to see homes with modern improvements surrounded by beautiful grassy lawns, flowers, shrubs and shade trees."

Julia did more than dream. Knowing that the city of her fantasies could not exist without more convenient transportation into and out of it, she renewed another former Cleveland connection in the form of James Ingraham, an employee of Henry Plant, who was building railroads on Florida's west coast. Ingraham oversaw a group of Plant's men who were charged with exploring the area to decide on the feasibility of running the railroad from Tampa to Fort Dallas. On one scouting trip, the party misjudged the dangers of the territory and was lost for twenty days before Julia prevailed upon Matlo to find them and conduct them to safety. After the Indian escorted the party safely back, Plant decided against building the railroad to the east coast and Matlo was not seen for several weeks. When he finally showed up again, he was missing an ear lobe. Unknown to Julia, the Seminoles considered it a major offense to conduct white men through Indian territory, and he had been banished for several weeks and visibly punished.

Julia, undeterred, turned her attention to Henry Flagler, who was completing his East Coast Railroad, terminating it at Palm Beach. Prevailing on their previous connection through Rockefeller, she wrote to him, proposing that if he would bring his railroad farther south to the tip of the peninsula, she would give him half her land. Before she could counter his polite but noncommittal answer, fate entered the picture.

On the night of December 28, 1894, the mercury fell precipitously, lingering in the teens and twenties most of the night. As far south as Jupiter, Florida, many families who had been earning their living growing citrus and truck farming were wiped out. Establishing citrus groves was a long process that took growers years of hard work before reaping any profits, but their misfortune was Julia's trump card.

To demonstrate that frost had not hit Miami, she sent Henry Flagler a gift box of fragrant orange blossoms packed in damp cotton. It was what he needed to convince him that his railroad should be extended past Palm Beach. As soon as it could be arranged, he visited Miami, signing Julia's contract, which gave him one hundred acres of her land to build a railroad terminal and a hotel. Julia reserved thirteen acres for herself and included the stipulation that nothing was to be built to interfere with her view of the bay. When the deal was done, she gave him a bonus of more land in interspersed, alternating parcels. If he wanted to develop his holdings, he would have to dig sewers, pave streets, and finance waterworks that would serve her real estate too.

Julia had learned her business lessons well in Cleveland. During the negotiations, she shrewdly asked the multimillionaire just how much stock he owned in the railroad company.

"Mrs. Tuttle," he replied, "I own that railroad as completely as I own this cigar or my umbrella. You have no cause to worry. The railroad will come to this spot."

"A woman of fire," Flagler later described the petite, feminine force who always wore black, even in the steamy, tropical summers.

When the big news leaked out and it became known that seven hundred workers were to be employed in building the hotel alone, men and their families flooded the area, camping out along the bay, surviving on meager rations, some nearly starving. Julia swung into action, building housing for the workers and, for good measure, the first laundry, the first bakery, and the first dairy for supplying milk to the hotel. Rents collected from her early undertakings provided the capital to buy more building materials, enabling her to continue increasing her investments.

There was little that escaped the touch of the "Mother of Miami." Although it was said Henry Flagler enjoyed an occasional alcoholic beverage, Julia was a strict prohibitionist. When she deeded her property to Flagler, he agreed not to allow liquor to be sold inside the city limits except at the bar at his Royal Palm Hotel during the three months of the tourist season.

As the settlement grew, the pro-whiskey men opened bars, some of them just twenty feet north of the city limits, naming the area North Miami. Along with whiskey, all sorts of vices flourished there—drunken fights, gambling, and shootings were daily occurrences. As many as three or four men might lie dead in the street after a night's revelry. Noisy dance halls were open half the night, and nothing could be done until some of the men decided to step over the line into Miami, where, at Julia's instigation, they were met by the sheriff. A battle ensued, with victory going to the Mother of Miami.

Before churches were built, Julia encouraged people to hold services in her parlor. She personally took a launch to West Palm Beach to bring back the Episcopal minister to conduct a service in Miami, and later she donated land for a church. Her pet parrot was said to have learned to sing the Doxology.

Under Julia's sharp eyes, surveying parties began their work, marking out streets that were much too narrow for the shining city of her vision. Complaining to Flagler produced no results. "The town will never be more than a fishing village for my hotel guests," he said.

J. E. Lummus, a businessman newcomer, told Julia he was anxious to build a badly needed general store, but since she was intercepting boats from Key West to buy their lumber, he wasn't able to get any. She promptly built the store for him, charging him twenty-five dollars a month rent. She did the same for others, including Miami's first doctor. There were no hard feelings. When Lummus became ill and no doctor was yet available, Julia nursed him back to health.

In April 1896, Henry Flagler's first railroad car pulled into Miami, by then a settlement of about fifteen hundred people. In three months, the town was officially incorporated as Miami, a Seminole word meaning "sweet water." Expansion began in earnest.

The city's first official Christmas was especially sweet to its hard-working citizens. They celebrated Christmas Eve with traditional church services, social gatherings, and family functions, topped off after dark by community fireworks. At four in the morning on Christmas Day, fire broke out near E. L. Brady's grocery store, spreading rapidly through adjacent wooden structures. Dressing quickly, Julia ran to the center of the action, where for hours she operated a heavy pump and helped pass buckets of water alongside the men.

When it was over, three blocks of commercial establishments had been incinerated. Some people believed the fire was a blessing in disguise since most of the buildings were the original wooden ones hastily constructed when the railroad came. Plans were made to replace them with brick ones.

Julia, who had gone overboard buying land and putting up buildings, was sinking deeper and deeper in debt. She was unhappy with the amount of help she was receiving from Flagler and developed severe, recurring headaches.

On the afternoon of September 14, 1898, at age forty-nine, she experienced a sudden, piercing headache. A woman friend who was staying with her at the time brought Julia a headache powder, but Julia was dead within the hour, almost certainly from a stroke.

Miami could hardly believe the news. A revered pioneer was dead. The headline in Miami's weekly newspaper, the *Metropolis,* proclaimed, "Miami's Most Prominent Citizen Goes to the Beyond."

Stores closed during the funeral services, and crowds of stunned citizens accompanied the procession to the new cemetery, where Julia's was the twelfth coffin interred.

"Surely Henry Flagler deserves all the credit he can get for building the railroad to Miami," said Florida Senator R. B. Gautier in 1959. "But he never lived in the jungle that Miami was in the 1890s as Mrs. Tuttle did. He never knew the hardships this lady did."

Others would add that, unlike Flagler, Plant, and the countless more who came later, there was no profit motive where Julia was concerned— only the vision of a beautiful city.

As early as 1896, Julia told a friend,

It will not be many years hence when Miami will be the most important port on the Atlantic Coast in the South. The time will come when the harbor and its approach will be dredged to a depth that will allow the deep sea-going vessels to anchor. Not only will this bring in the coastwise steamers, whose captains now cast longing eyes toward Miami as they pass, but the South American vessels will finally ply between their home ports and Miami, and Miami will become the great center in all the southland. This may seem far-fetched to you, but as surely as the sun rises and sets all of this will come true.

And it did. Julia's vision came true.

MARY MCLEOD BETHUNE

1875–1955

DAUGHTER OF SLAVES,
ADVISER TO PRESIDENTS

Fourth of July celebrations were special in the McLeod family, particularly after the Emancipation. The big family gathered for a picnic and reunion to celebrate the birth of the nation on the fourth, Mary Jane's birthday on the tenth, sister Sallie's birthday on the fourth, and baby sister Hattie's birthday on the twelfth. Mary Jane's father sometimes took her with him to the market in Mayesville, South Carolina, the next day, as an added treat.

She loved being in the bustling market, helping Papa sell his eggs, shopping for new tools, and, of course, it was always a treat to lunch alone with Papa. After one of those lunches, they joined the crowd behind the store for a horse show. By that time of day some men had had too much to drink, and after lighting a cigarette, one white man ordered a black man to blow out his match. When the black man refused, there was a nasty struggle. Mary Jane didn't understand what was happening, but her stomach felt icy and her heart pounded.

Grasping her hand, Papa rushed her away to their wagon, but still she heard ugly voices and shouts. "Git the rope!" "Haul 'im up!"

Papa wouldn't let her look back as they got away as fast as their old mule would run. She could see by Papa's face that something terrible had happened, but she knew not to ask questions. The day that started out so fine was ruined. For the first time ever, she knew bad things could happen anywhere and to anyone, and even Papa could be scared and couldn't fix everything.

Mary McLeod Bethune   Florida State Archives

Mary Jane McLeod was born on July 10, 1875, the fifteenth of seventeen children born to Samuel and Patsy McLeod. Patsy, although illiterate, spoke softly, carrying herself with the dignity expected from one said to be descended from African royalty. Samuel was a farmer, a skilled carpenter, and a tin and leather worker. They were married before the Emancipation. Some of their older children were born into slavery and sold to nearby landowners, but they all managed to reassemble after President Lincoln's Proclamation. Although Mary Jane was born free, she was no stranger to the evils of slavery.

In the hard-working family, everyone had to do his or her part. Patsy tended sick neighbors with herbs, sometimes delivering babies, for money if her patients had any, for nothing if they didn't. Mary eventually learned to cook, sew, and chop cotton. She sang as she worked in the fields and in the Methodist Episcopal church where the family worshipped and where her parents were officers. They all worked the farm, praying together every night and morning.

Mostly, Mary prayed to be able to go to school. More than anything, she wanted to read. One of her friends, the white daughter of a sharecropper, had books that fascinated her. Once when Mary picked a book up to examine it, the girl told her to put it down. "You can't read," she said. "Put it down." After that, as she worked in the fields, Mary prayed to be able to go to school. She eagerly attended a new church school.

Mary did so well at her studies that after graduating, she was awarded a scholarship to Scotia Seminary in North Carolina. In 1887 she left her family to ride alone on a train, frightened but proud, to her new school where unknown worlds opened. She made friends with people from strange places and ate strange foods with utensils she had never before seen. Like a sponge, she absorbed everything.

After graduation from Scotia, she continued her education at the Moody Bible Institute in Chicago, the one African American in a school of a thousand students, and her world expanded again. Walking the city streets to pass out literature and spread the word of God, sometimes alone in the meanest areas, she was threatened more than once, but her faith sustained her. There were successes, too, such as when some of the street toughs returned with her to the mission to pursue a new life.

She then taught in mission schools in Georgia for a year and in Sumter, South Carolina. While singing in a choir there, handsome, young Albertus Bethune caught her eye. Having given up teaching due to the poor pay, he was working in a men's clothing department in order to contribute money to finance his brother's college education. He and Mary met frequently at choir practice. He taught her to ride a bicycle, and on their long rides together, they fell in love.

After a year's courtship, they were married in May 1898 and moved to Savannah, Georgia, where Albertus had a promising opportunity in the menswear business. In 1899 baby Albertus McLeod Bethune was born. By the time her son was nine months old, Mary was anxious to resume teaching. She and her husband started a mission school in Palatka, Florida, the state she would call home for the rest of her life.

She spent four hectic years getting the new school off to a good start, and, as it began to grow, she allowed herself to dream her private dream of establishing her own school for African-American girls, whose low social status, she believed, could never be corrected without proper education.

Drawn to Daytona by its climate, by the need to educate the great numbers of children of working men employed in the construction of Henry Flagler's railroad, and by the influx of well-to-do tourists who might be a source of income, she decided to try to fulfill her dream there.

She found a small frame house a few blocks from the railroad. It rented for eleven dollars a month, but the landlord agreed to accept her offer of one dollar and fifty cents plus the rest at the end of the month. She made good on her promise by baking sweet potato pies and selling them to workmen for their noon meal.

For school supplies, she combed the city dump and trash piles behind resort hotels, salvaging cracked dishes, lamps, brooms, and discarded furniture. Packing crates became desks for her students, and charred wood served as pencils.

On October 3, 1904, the Daytona Educational and Industrial Training School for Negro Girls opened its doors. Five little girls and her own five-year-old son trooped in past the founder and sole teacher to begin their scholastic careers with a hymn and a psalm.

Mary soon saw there was a need to board some students, those whose mothers were maids and necessarily left for periods of time with their white employers. She rescued a cast-off bed, painted it, and had three girls sleep crosswise on it the first night. Her boarders lived mostly on black-eyed peas and hominy grits, but they were grateful for the opportunity to learn.

When neighbors began showing up, interested in the school doings, Mary realized they were illiterate and offered to provide evening classes for them if they would supply lanterns to illuminate the classrooms.

Her school grew faster than she could keep up. Before long, the original building was too small, but with so many students paying tuition in eggs or chickens, there was never enough money for the necessities, let alone a bigger building. Much of Mary's time and energy was taken up soliciting funds from wealthy tourists. One who would be important in her life and in the lives of the school's first pupils was James Gamble, of the Procter and Gamble firm in Cincinnati, Ohio, a winter resident so impressed with the school, he made an immediate sizable cash donation.

At her invitation, he and several other prominent Daytona citizens visited the classes, where they were deeply moved by what she had accomplished with so few resources. Mr. Gamble was the first to agree to her request to form a board of trustees.

Besides academic studies, Mary taught her students cleanliness, pride of surroundings, and elementary housekeeping, enabling older girls to work in wealthy households while they took classes, in order to pay for clothing and other necessities. She was criticized for this in some circles. One black preacher railed from the pulpit, attacking her for teaching girls to be servants, but she was adamant. "There is no such thing as menial work," she said, "only menial spirit."

She also insisted on teaching music, leading the student choir with her own fine voice. As they improved, she took the group to hotels, providing guests with entertainment, and then giving a talk about what the school was accomplishing. Someone invariably passed a basket, contributing immeasurably to the never-ending task of finding funds.

As word spread, more wealthy people became interested. C. C. Mellour, owner of Pittsburgh's largest music store, heard the choir and was so moved, he bought the school a fine, new grand piano and often paid outstanding bills thereafter.

The need for more space, including a dormitory, was becoming imperative. As money became available, a new building, Faith Hall, was constructed and moved into in 1907, although it was still unfinished. Mary insisted on having running water, annoying the contractor who said "Nigras" didn't need such things as bathrooms. She held her ground, and, as a result, the entire African-American section of Daytona had city water piped in for the first time.

Another new friend was Thomas H. White, owner of White Sewing Machines and White Steamer Automobiles in Cleveland, Ohio. On his tour through Faith Hall, he saw unplastered walls, nearly empty shelves where food was usually stored to feed the boarders, and in a corner, a rickety Singer sewing machine. He left a generous check before departing and then sent workmen to install floors, windows, plumbing, and wiring, finishing the building at his expense, and soon, a brand new White sewing machine arrived on the premises. He was one of the school's benefactors for the rest of his life, chiefly responsible, at Mary's prodding, for the installation of electric lines and a sewage system in the African-American part of town.

Weekly Sunday afternoon community meetings were held in the school's assembly room, increasingly drawing the town's citizens, white and black. Mary refused to permit "preferred seating" for whites, as was customary in the South. This practice led to the school becoming an informal exchange for interracial culture and understanding. As word of the school spread, the number of Mary's speaking engagements increased, sometimes sponsored by well-to-do tourists. By 1909, she had to hire an educational director in order to concentrate solely on business and administration.

At age thirty-five, she spoke before the National Association of Colored Women, the largest such organization in the country. From South Carolina State College she received the first of the eleven honorary degrees she would accumulate.

With her increasing involvement in the school and other attempts at elevating her race, she and Albertus grew further apart. In 1908 he disappeared from her life, and they never saw each other again. He returned to South Carolina, contracted tuberculosis, and died in 1919.

Her friends White and Gamble bought a small cottage for her near the school, allowing her some privacy and respite from the chattering girls she loved but needed to escape from occasionally. It was named the Retreat.

As her familiarity with the city of Daytona grew, so, too, did her determination to reach out to all its citizens. Seeing African-American boys idling in the streets inspired her to start a boys' club, where boys could read, play games, and interact, much as white boys did at the YMCA.

In a crucial 1920 election, one big issue influencing the opposing candidates for mayor was a bill providing for the first public high school for African-American children. One candidate was backed by the Ku Klux Klan; the other strongly favored the school and backed improvements in the African-American section of Daytona.

Mary held meetings in Faith Hall, urging ministers and others of influence to call on parishioners, arouse them to register to vote if they hadn't, and to vote. Some longtime citizens warned her of possible dangers, but Mary persisted, calling on all black and white friends. "Don't be afraid of the Klan," she said. "Look every man straight in the eye and make no apology to anyone because of race or color. When you see a burning cross, remember the Son of God who bore the heaviest cross of all!"

About ten o'clock on the night before the election, the politically powerful Klan had the streetlights turned off in the African-American section of town before they began their march toward Mary's school, the sounds of horses' hooves and trumpets heralding their arrival. A burning cross preceded the line of white hoods as they progressed through the school's gate toward the frightened, watching girls. At that point, Mary ordered the school-controlled lights turned off inside and the outside campus lights turned on, illuminating the terrorists. Through the hush came the sound of one student's brave voice, quavering but insistent, the words of a hymn ringing out in the still air. "Be not dismayed whate'er betide. God will take care of us." The tables were reversed, and the white-hooded horde disappeared into the blackness. The Klan's favored candidate lost the election.

When the school was seven years old, the need for a high school was obvious to many, but not to Mary's board of trustees. Until she threatened to leave to start another school, they resisted her plan to start a high school. But finally her old friend Gamble threw his support to her, and the school became a reality, graduating the first class in 1915. In addition, she started a library and a tiny hospital, which grew rapidly to include twenty-six beds and eventually became a school for practical nurses.

With the start of World War I in 1914, U.S. vice president Thomas Marshall invited Mary to Washington to confer on the possibility of restructuring the Red Cross as a desegregated organization. Hurriedly making repairs to her wardrobe, which consisted of donated clothing from missionary barrels, she traveled to the capital, making such an eloquent plea that her people be allowed to serve as others did in humanitarian tasks, the Red Cross was integrated. She was then sent on a speaking tour to recruit for that organization and was put in charge of her local chapter, headquartered in West Palm Beach.

Her first love was and always would be the school, but she realized she needed more secure financial backing than she had had previously. She declined public aid, refusing to put the school under the control of Florida legislators and similarly rebuffing support from the Catholic Church, determined as she was to maintain religious control and a nondenominational code. In 1923 she agreed to merge with the Cookman Institute, a school for boys in Jacksonville, under the auspices of the Methodist Church, but with the agreement that she would maintain full policy control, including remaining nondenominational. Her little school had grown into Bethune-Cookman College.

As president of the State Federation of Colored Women's Clubs, she used her influence to set up the first home for wayward girls in Florida and increased her visibility by meeting with white women's clubs. In 1927 hers was the only dark face among invited guests at a luncheon given by Eleanor Roosevelt for woman leaders in New York. Noting the uneasy glances of Southern women, Eleanor's mother-in-law, Sara Roosevelt, took Mary's arm and sat her at the right hand of the future president's wife, beginning a close, personal friendship among the three women.

In 1928, while Mary was involved in transforming her school into a junior college, she received an invitation from President Calvin Coolidge to attend a Child Welfare Conference. There were no outstanding results from the conference, but it served to highlight children's issues and led to Mary's attendance at a similar commission under Herbert Hoover. She was becoming the country's expert on education of African Americans.

President Roosevelt inaugurated the National Youth Administration in 1935 with Mary McLeod Bethune as its administrator, the first time a federal post was created for an African-American woman. She got along famously with President Roosevelt, speaking to him, as she once said, "as the voice of fourteen million Americans who seek to achieve full citizenship. We have been taking the crumbs for a long time. We have been eating the feet and the head of the chicken long enough. The time has come when we want some white meat."

That same year, the National Association for the Advancement of Colored People (NAACP) awarded her a gold medal for "the highest or noblest achievement by an American Negro."

When the United States entered World War II, Mary campaigned successfully to have African-American women admitted to the Women's Army Auxiliary Corps. She lent her name to many causes, some in sincere efforts to seek peace with the Soviet Union, resulting in her being investigated by the FBI, although subsequently cleared of wrongdoing. She also spoke out forcefully and frequently against lynching.

In 1945, in what she considered her crowning achievement, President Truman named her a consultant to the conference drafting the United Nations charter, enabling her to help make a difference for her people around the world. She realized another lifelong dream when President Truman made her a delegate to Liberia's presidential inauguration, allowing her to spend eight arduous but inspiring days in Africa.

Exhausted and suffering from recurrent asthma and heart disease, she was hospitalized for three months after she returned. She then moved into the expanded Retreat where she spent the rest of her days, surrounded by her growing collection of honors, family, and friends. To anyone who inquired about her health, she always answered, "I'm wonderful!"

She died quietly on May 18, 1955, leaving a last will and testament to all her people:

I leave you love.

I leave you hope.

I leave you a thirst for education.

I leave you faith.

I leave you racial dignity.

I leave you a desire to live harmoniously with your fellow men.

I leave you finally a responsibility to our young people.

HARRIET BEDELL

1875–1969

WHITE SISTER OF THE SEMINOLES

Harriet Bedell accompanied her friends through the rear door of a Miami curio shop, following the signs to view a "genuine Indian village," where inhabitants were "engaged in going about their daily business." What she saw sickened her.

"I was appalled," she said. "I believe it's all right to exhibit arts and crafts, but not people." And that surely was happening.

As white tourists gawked beneath a placard proclaiming "alligator wrestling," Indian men poked at old alligators, trying to arouse hostility in the animals. Bored women dressed in shabby imitation Seminole costumes simulated domestic chores, while children posed for photographs. Even the totem pole was a pathetic fake, and Harriet was certain the curios in the shop had been manufactured in Newark or some such place.

Impetuously, she offered her hand to an Indian man, saying, "I am a friend of the Indian. Hello." He stared at her a moment then walked away. She then approached a woman, touching her shoulder lightly, speaking the same way. The woman looked through her as though she wasn't there, shrugged Harriet's hand from her shoulder, and strolled off.

It was 1933 and Deaconess Harriet Bedell was officially retired, but she decided on the spot that she would request assignment to the Seminole Indians of Florida. With all her heart, she believed they were deserving of dignity, and she wanted to help assure their dignity was respected.

"There's no retirement in the Master's work," she told the bishop when she asked to be allowed to reopen the closed Glades Cross Mission as a volunteer. After his reply that there was no money for it, she

Harriet Bedell   Florida State Archives

offered to use her vacation money. She would need a car, he said. She'd get one, she answered. Could she drive? She would learn.

The bishop discovered, as so many others had, that it was not easy to win an argument with the tiny, frail-looking woman in her neat, blue habit.

Harriet was born March 19, 1875, in Buffalo, New York, the oldest of three children; Sarah, nicknamed Sadie, came next, then Alfred, called Allie.

Their father, Horace Ira Bedell, came from a family of boatmen and ran his own excursion boat that circled Grand Island in the Niagara River. He also invested in canal boats in New York State.

Their mother, Louisa Sophia Oberest, was a Swiss beauty known for her intellect and talent at guitar playing.

The Bedell family's comfortable life ended in 1885 when Horace fell overboard and drowned, leaving behind debts incurred in the financial crash of 1884. Louisa was forced to sell the family home and most of their furniture and make do with a small rental home. She taught all her children to cook, to be frugal, and to prepare themselves to earn their own living. "You must never ask for or accept help except from God," she impressed on them.

Harriet graduated from State Normal School in Buffalo in 1894, taught in a one-room school on Grand Island for a year, and then advanced in the public school system until she became an assistant principal. Parties, picnics, hayrides, and sleigh rides enlivened Harriet's life, and she took part in social evenings at a resort on Grand Island owned by her uncle, Ossian Bedell. Contributing to the family finances and teaching Sunday school at St. Mary's, the Protestant Episcopal church where the family worshiped, was gratifying, but she wanted to do more with her life.

The words of a visiting missionary at one Sunday morning service describing the suffering of multitudes of Chinese people, in desperate need of food and education, affected Harriet as nothing else she could recall. A realistic, intelligent young woman, she refused to say her experience was any sort of divine calling; she only knew the urge to act was overpowering. She wanted to go to China to do what she could to help.

In 1901 she applied for and was accepted for a two-year course at the Training School for Deaconesses in New York City. She studied the Bible, church history, teaching methods, hygiene, bookkeeping, and religious music and prepared meals for the sick. She also trained for a year in hospital nursing at the General Hospital in Buffalo, working along-side nurses for two weeks in each ward.

Bowing to her mother's objections, Harriet reluctantly gave up the idea of going to China. She was instead assigned to the Whirlwind Mission in the Oklahoma Territory where she would work among the Cheyenne Indians, some of whom had participated in the Indian death march to Yellowstone following their defeat in 1868 at the hands of Custer. Harriet, under no illusions that her job would be an easy one, would earn a salary of four hundred dollars a year.

Harriet traveled to Oklahoma and immediately set to work. With her incredible energy, she established a school and a chapel that grew to be St. Luke's Church; and, after one year, she had so earned the respect and admiration of the Cheyenne, they made her a member of their tribe and presented her with a splendid Indian gown, symbolizing that they considered her a woman of high rank. At the great feast that followed, she was given the name "Vicsehia," meaning "Bird Woman," because she sang as she worked. She spent eight of the most satisfying years of her life among the Cheyenne, surviving temperatures of up to 115 degrees in summer, teaching, working, and learning.

But in 1915 she contracted tuberculosis, a particularly widespread disease among Indians. Arrangements were made for her to journey to Denver, where the mountain air was expected to be helpful but where Harriet was convinced she was going to die. While there, she attended a "healing service" at a nearby church, after which, against all medical expectations, her skin tests, repeated again and again, proved negative for tuberculosis. She rejected claiming a miracle, but she was immensely grateful for her good fortune and even more determined to spend her life in service to others. She was sent to Stevens Village in Alaska, forty miles below the Arctic Circle, where she quickly forgot the heat of Oklahoma.

In fact, she froze her nose once when the temperature dropped to seventy degrees below zero and a freshly made cup of steaming tea carried twenty paces had ice formed on top. When there were only a few hours of daylight out of every twenty-four-hour period, she became so confused using a revised, outdated calendar, she sometimes lost whole days and even weeks.

Unquestionably, her most grueling ordeal was a 1918 dogsled trip with two guides over an unbroken trail to take a small, sick girl to a doctor. The temperature was thirty-two degrees below zero when they started the journey. Harriet took brief rests on the sled with the child but mostly snowshoed with the men. When the crusty old owner of one cabin where they stopped for the night saw her, he said, "A woman! Lady, I wouldn't have been more s'prised if a skunk came over that trail draggin' a bear by the tail!" Harriet politely turned down his invitation to marriage "when the ice goes out." In all, she traveled 160 miles to take the child to the amazed doctor, who diagnosed polio. Happily, the girl recovered.

In September of 1922, before returning to Buffalo on furlough, Harriet attended a General Convention of the church in Portland, Oregon, where she was at long last consecrated as a deaconess. The experience was so solemn and moving that she gave up in frustration when she attempted to record it in a diary. She could never put into words what it meant to be then and forever "Deaconess Bedell."

The trip back to New York was exciting and she cherished the time with her family, but she longed to be "home" with "her" Indians.

Life in Alaska, always difficult for Indians, grew even worse during the Great Depression. While sources of funding dried up, the Indian economy was rapidly breaking down from the overfishing and overhunting necessary to sustain production in the canneries. Harriet constantly raided her own food supply to help others.

In 1930 Harriet was given a furlough to spend some time with her mother after Alfred's death and then to make fundraising speeches. The work took her to New York, Philadelphia, Pittsburgh, Massachusetts,

Miami, Ohio, and Connecticut. It was while she was in Miami that she became horrified at the exhibitions of people as crass entertainment.

She set about learning some of the history of the Seminole people, especially the Mikasuki Tribe and those who refused to live on the reservations. She heard about the three Seminole wars and how the Seminoles had been repeatedly tricked and betrayed by white men. She learned that Spain and the United States had signed agreements on ownership of lands that belonged to the Indians, and that even after the Indians agreed to leave their old lands for new ones, whites encroached on those new lands. She found out that Osceola, the great Seminole leader, had been massacred while attending a parley under a flag of truce.

Obviously, some things could never be reversed. Harriet knew the past could not be changed. But she also knew that whites would continue pressing, inexorably crowding in on the Seminoles, who would have to make accommodations or be overwhelmed, perhaps eradicated. With her past Indian experience, Harriet was certain she could help. She did not know how; she only knew she ached to do something.

After Harriet received the church's permission and the endorsement of the federal Indian agent for her venture, the County Operating Company provided her with a rental house in Everglades City, the company town owned and operated by Barron Collier. He owned most of the land in Collier County and was also a power behind the construction of the Tamiami Trail, the narrow highway that linked the Florida coasts through the Everglades and Big Cypress Swamp, areas alive with bears, panthers, snakes, and alligators.

Another benefactor provided funds for a used Model A Ford, and within a week, Harriet was driving, although she never drove faster than thirty-five miles an hour, frequently infuriating other drivers behind her on the Tamiami Trail.

The car was necessary to reach the Indians, the Mikasukis being considered among the more intransigent tribes, as attested to by the facts that they had never signed a peace treaty with the United States and most had stubbornly refused to live on reservations. Instead, they lived in scattered villages along the Trail.

Harriet learned that Barron Collier owned about a million acres, or 90 percent, of the county that bore his name. According to his spokesman, David Copeland, Collier also voluntarily assumed 90 percent of the responsibility for the county and paid 90 percent of the bills. Harriet established immediate rapport with Copeland, who told her, "These are mighty strange Indians. They neither like us nor hate us. For the most part, they act as if we just aren't there."

Recalling his words, Harriet drove to a nearby Seminole village for her first attempt at forming a friendship. There was no overt hostility on the part of the Indians; they simply acted as if she were invisible. She struggled to hide her hurt, trying at another village the next day. Again she was stonily ignored. She continued the discouraging routine day after day in one village, then another, until, finally after about two months, a Seminole man grunted when she spoke to him as they passed in the street—a triumph!

As she went about her business, Harriet was learning, and one fact was inescapable. The Great Depression, which had wreaked havoc on whites, was more devastating by far to the Indians. Tourism had become nearly nonexistent, and without it, no money came from selling handicrafts. There was little farm work to speak of and there were few animals to hunt. The solution to the problem would become her largest single project among the Seminoles. With the encouragement of her bishop and the backing of the County Operating Company, she crafted her plan.

In order to spread her message, she spent two entire days waiting in her car on the same street where the man had grunted in response to her greeting. When he finally appeared, she hailed him as a friend and appealed to him to listen to her ideas.

She asked him to tell the Seminoles to bring their handiwork, shirts, skirts, and carvings, anything of good quality, and she would give them a fair price. She would then sell the materials to churches and other contacts she had around the country, without taking any fee. All the profits would belong to the Seminoles. The man understood and agreed.

Within a week, the first Indians came to her with their articles, and the following morning one of them returned in his car to drive her deep into the Everglades to a Mikasuki village where Deaconess Bedell experienced firsthand the beauties of the Grassy Water. She gave her first religious instruction to a polite audience. "They're a very polite people," she said. "Unusually tolerant of religions similar to their own." She said they believed in a Great Spirit. "So do I." It was a beginning.

As she and the Indians grew to know each other, mutual respect developed, and within a year, Indians appeared regularly at her mission with their handicrafts. The deaconess became a familiar figure in the villages, driving, hiking, canoeing, or wading, whatever it took, to reach someone in need.

She conducted services and sewing classes, made sick calls, and handled increasing numbers of tourists. She taught hygiene and urged the Seminoles to bury their wastes. She tried to convey the advantage of eating from separate bowls and spoons rather than the common ones that were customary in their culture. As the sales of handicrafts increased, there was bookkeeping to attend to and correspondence that never ended. She helped find work for young men and scolded them if they drank too much.

"You can't live with people without loving them," she said.

When she received word of her mother's death while attending a convention in Atlantic City in 1934, she sent words of consolation to her sister and remained where she was. "My sister knows I grieve as much as she does," she said. "My work is not in Buffalo. It's here . . . and in Florida with the Indians."

In 1936 Harriet held the first of what would become her annual Christmas feasts in one of the villages. About seventy-five Indians attended the services during which she explained the significance of the day and of the gifts that followed. Together, they sang carols and consumed one hundred pounds of meat and all the trimmings.

During the festivities, Harriet learned of a new problem looming for the Seminoles. Along with restrictive new gaming laws, they nervously faced the proposed establishment of Everglades National Park, with the resulting loss of more than 1,200,000 acres of hunting lands. "I strongly approve of the park project," she said, speaking out wherever she could. "But these Indians must somehow be drawn into the white economy or at least be given the same chance for survival that we're offering the animals in the park plan!"

When a 1937 flu epidemic hit the tribe, Harriet cared for fourteen Indians at the Glades Cross Mission, catching what little sleep she could on a cot on a porch. It was a grueling ordeal but produced its reward when the patients got well and were paid a visit by the medicine man. He called her "In-co-shopie" (woman of God) and pronounced her his sister. "You are my brother," she answered in return.

Harriet was sixty-three in 1938 when she lost her last family member. Sadie died and was followed shortly by Barron Collier, who had become Harriet's good friend. She grieved, prayed, and increased her rounds of work.

She held religious services on Marco Island for the families of commercial fishermen and at the county jail for the prisoners. At the close of her long days, she still had enough energy to knit squares for afghans to be sold for emergency money wherever it might be needed.

In 1943 Harriet was forced into official retirement but was permitted to continue working as a volunteer, and she carried on in her usual energetic fashion. Typically, the Mikasukis trusted no white person but the deaconess to sign their ration cards, and they declared war on the Axis as a separate nation.

In 1947, Harriet was honored to give the invocation for the dedication of Everglades National Park, lunching afterward with President Harry Truman and other notables.

As her fame spread, she was dismayed to hear some people describe her as a saint. "Rubbish!" she said. She was simply a woman and a cranky one at that, she declared.

Her ire came again to the forefront when Seminoles related their latest tale of woe. White hunters were being hired to kill deer supposedly infected with ticks that destroyed white men's cattle. Why, the Seminoles asked, did the Indians' deer have to be killed to save the white men's cattle? Even the Audubon Society and many white hunters agreed the tick would survive the slaughter, and that fencing and dipping were the answer. She agreed with them, but writing letters, speaking out, and praying were all she could do about it.

On October 7, 1960, Hurricane Donna tore through the Everglades. Eighty-five-year-old Harriet weathered the disaster at the home of a friend. When calm returned, Glades Mission House was gone, as were all her personal things—letters, books, typewriter, sewing machine, all gone. Her missionary career was necessarily over, since there was no money to rebuild the mission at the time, the authorities said. But there was a place for her at the Bishop Gray Inn for retired missionaries in Davenport, Florida. Sensibly, she agreed to go there but let it be known she would hold her annual Christmas feast as usual. Over 150 people attended the celebration that year.

Even in retirement at Davenport, the devout dynamo brought comfort to other retirees who were less fortunate physically, and she never failed to include them in her prayers just as she did her beloved Seminoles.

The White Sister of the Seminoles died in Davenport in January 1969 at the age of ninety-three and was buried at nearby Haines City.

Eartha M. M. White

1876–1971

ANGEL OF MERCY

On Friday, May 3, 1901, the cloudless skies over Jacksonville were brilliant blue. The air was calm as workers from the Cleaveland Fiber Factory broke for lunch outdoors, relaxing close to some moss that had been spread out to dry in the sun. Sparks wafted into the air from the chimney of a nearby shanty where food was being prepared. Suddenly some of the sparks landed on piles of moss, setting them on fire. Seeing the glow, a worker rushed for a bucket of water, saw more sparks and more smoldering fibers, and shouted for help. Wind rose in sudden gusts, propelling flames into the warehouse. Within minutes, the entire wooden building was afire, its roof caving in, hurling pieces of burning shingles and moss in all directions, setting more fires everywhere the debris fell.

There had been no rain for over a month, and as the wind continued to swirl eastward, a wall of fire set the wooden houses, churches, and shops of Jacksonville ablaze. It then split to form another wall that roared westward, consuming other commercial buildings, the courthouse, the post office, and a structure containing ammunition and dynamite, which exploded, adding to the terrible inferno. Highways jammed with people trying to escape. Towering black smoke could be seen as far away as Savannah, Georgia. Firefighters from Savannah rushed to join others from Fernandina and St. Augustine to help the exhausted men in Jacksonville. By half past eight that night, as the last embers were extinguished, the city was a scene of total devastation, with 146 city blocks having vanished, 2,368 buildings gone. Miraculously, just 7 lives were lost, but 8,677 people were left homeless and destitute.

Eartha M. M. White   Eartha White Collection, Thomas G. Carpenter Library, University of North Florida

Reporters from all over the country poured into Jacksonville, and a young man from Baltimore, H. L. Mencken, reporting from the heart of the city, wrote:

Today the ruins stand like Pompeii-tall spires of crumbling brick and hillocks of cracked and powdered stone. Ordinarily a burned house appears as a smoky shell with black and dampened interior. But in the ruins of Jacksonville there is no trace of black, for the fire burned everything that was burnable, and when it was gone and its work was done, there remain white ashes and swirling dust. In the place of these white ashes and stumps of walls there stood, 10 days ago, about $15,000,000 worth of houses. Today they are worth 10 cents a carload, delivered at the dump.

Almost all public papers were lost, but during the conflagration, Eartha M. M. White loaded a cart with valuable records and rushed them to safety in the suburbs. Then, without pausing, she set to work with her mother, Clara, to feed, clothe, and comfort as many acquaintances and strangers as she could from her own home, an oasis still standing amidst the nightmare of terror and fatigue in the city.

They continued their work tirelessly, day after day, giving life to the motto Clara taught her daughter and which Eartha adopted and would follow all her life: "Do all the good you can, in all the ways you can, for all the people you can, while you can."

Eartha Mary Magdalene White, a native Floridian, was born on November 8, 1876, the daughter of a young black woman, Mollie Chapman, and a young white man from a prominent family. Eartha was adopted by Clara White soon after birth and was unaware of her real parentage for years. Eartha later learned her real father's identity but chose never to reveal it to anyone.

Clara, a fervent humanitarian and deeply religious woman, named the baby girl Eartha because "everything you get comes from the earth," and gave her the middle name Mary Magdalene after the good woman of the Bible.

Clara had been born a slave on Amelia Island and lived with the memory of seeing her own mother sold away before her eyes when Clara was a small child. She grew up serving white masters until she was freed by the Emancipation. Soon after, she married Lafayette White. He died when Eartha was just five years old, leaving Clara alone to care for her daughter. Working as a hotel maid and steamboat stewardess, she still managed to help others, even furnishing Christmas stockings for poor neighborhood children.

Clara and Eartha formed a lasting, loving relationship, dedicated to doing good. With her mother as a role model, it was not surprising that Eartha would become Jacksonville's first African-American social worker.

Eartha attended Stanton School and the Divinity School, graduating in 1893, just as Jacksonville was quarantined for yellow fever. To protect her daughter, Clara sent Eartha to New York City to stay with friends, and while there, she attended the Madam Hall Beauty School and the National Conservatory of Music, which led to her being accepted as lyric soprano with the Oriental American Opera Company. This organization, said to be the first black opera company in the United States, was financed by a man from Syracuse, New York, who wanted to prove "that Negroes could sing music other than folk songs." The company's opening at the Palmer Theater on Broadway in New York in 1896 was highly successful, and Eartha traveled widely with the company in the United States and Europe for over a year.

During intermittent trips home, she met and fell in love with a railroad worker named James Jordan, and they planned a Jacksonville wedding for June 1896. During her absences they wrote to each other often, but gradually, his letters to her related the onset and progression of an illness, his loss of weight and gradual weakness, until she was notified in May that he had died while she was touring. Grieving, she returned home to Jacksonville, where the twenty-year-old abruptly changed directions, giving up her musical career and choosing instead to join her mother in a life of service to others.

After graduating from the Florida Baptist Academy in 1897, she took a year in Jacksonville to care for the sick and wounded of the Spanish-American War before securing a teaching assignment to a one-room school in Bayard, ten miles to the south. She transferred the following year to Stanton School, where she taught for fifteen years. She managed to excel at her teaching career while working in the evenings at the African American Insurance Company, a leading financial center for Jacksonville's black population and a sponsor of scholarly and humanitarian causes. It was the African American Insurance Company records Eartha saved in the great fire of 1901, consequently providing financial relief for some families.

She and Clara also raised funds to establish a Colored Old Folks Home in 1902 and worked to resurrect the defunct Union Benevolent Association to get badly needed help for poor blacks.

At the same time, Eartha displayed sharp business sense, opening a dry goods store in 1905 with $150, building it up, and selling it in 1913 for $10,000. She did the same with a housecleaning and employment bureau, a taxi company, and a steam laundry with the memorable motto: "Put your duds in our suds, we wash anything but a dirty conscience." Later in life, she would laugh at her youthful ignorance when she began her business ventures, but she was always a fast learner, and eventually, she even became a licensed real estate broker. As a result of her business dealings, she joined and attended the first meeting of the National Negro Business League in Boston in 1900, where she met Booker T. Washington and was influenced by his philosophy of personal diplomacy and appeal to the moral consciences of whites.

But always, there was time and indeed a need within herself to help those less fortunate—orphans, alcoholics, the aged, handicapped, unwed mothers, the downtrodden in general.

For many years after the Old Folks Home was operational, she took upon herself the thankless task of acquiring funds to provide all the vital essentials for its residents. Next, she helped organize the City Federation of Women's Clubs, which, like the white Woman's Club in Jacksonville, concerned itself with children, young women, health, suffrage, education, the court system, and the arts. In cooperation with white women's clubs, the Federation joined in community celebrations, honoring heroes of both races.

Eartha and Mary McLeod Bethune became long-distance friends, working for some of the same causes, but the two women had entirely different styles of leadership. Just five feet tall, Eartha was soft-spoken and although strong, she was "not overly assertive." She became known as Jacksonville's "Angel of Mercy," but by the same token, one Jacksonville politician was quoted as saying, "Sometimes I hate to see her coming. I know she's going to try to touch me for a lot more than I want to give—and I know she's going to get it!"

Another time, Mayor Hans Tanzler said, "At least once a month she'd come to my office at City Hall. She was irrepressible and undeniable. . . . She only came up to my waist, but she'd point that little finger at me and she'd tell me, 'God has chosen you and you must do this, that and the other thing.' I called her my black angel and she was an angel in every true sense of the word. She lived for other people. Every nickel she could get went to help others."

When delinquency among black boys was beginning to be a problem in 1904, her answer was to form a Boys' Improvement Club to fight idleness. She then established a park where children could play, paying the salaries of its employees herself for ten years until the city took over the responsibility. Afterward, she turned her attention to girls, gently applying pressure on state legislators in a push for a facility to be built for delinquent girls. She managed regular visits to the institutions she was influential in starting, always encouraging, compassionate, and bearing in mind her mother's motto.

As part of her extensive work at the county jail, for fifty years Eartha led a Sunday school for the inmates, arranging religious activities and counseling services, and taking cigars and other small gifts to the often forgotten men.

Saying "much too much importance is given to the color of the skin in this world of ours," she assisted the downtrodden of all races, according dignity to all.

In time she was largely responsible for establishing a home for unwed mothers, a Tuberculosis Rest Home, and an orphanage for African-American children. In 1902 she solicited funds to establish a badly needed nursing home for senior African Americans.

Certainly, the project nearest and dearest to Eartha's heart was the Clara White Mission, begun as a soup kitchen by Clara in the 1880s. The mission never turned anyone away, whatever the color of his or her skin.

When World War I broke out, Eartha added numerous patriotic activities to her already crowded schedule. She was instrumental in organizing Red Cross programs and took charge of the War Camp Community Services, Southern Division in Savannah, Georgia, which aided both servicemen and their families in times of crisis. When President Woodrow Wilson convened a Council on National Defense at the White House, Eartha was honored to be the only black person in attendance. The daughter of slaves could not help but reflect on how far she had come.

The war brought on shortages in foods and fuels, making it necessary to educate the public about food substitutes and methods of conserving fuels. She and other black club women established Liberty Kitchen at a local high school to teach women these skills.

During the war, employment opportunities not previously available opened for young black women, and Eartha was there to assist them in seizing those opportunities. To ensure they would not be exploited, she hastily organized a Mutual Protection League for Working Girls, which was highly praised for its effectiveness and fairness.

Two years into the war saw Jacksonville hit by still another calamity—the onset of a raging flu epidemic in 1918. Beginning at the city prison farm, it spread quickly, and by October, the city health officer published health warnings in the newspapers, calling for Jacksonville citizens to stay at home. The official closed all schools and recreational facilities. Public gatherings were forbidden, and even churches and synagogues were closed or strictly limited to holding funeral services for families only. Along with these closures and the restrictions on store hours, downtown Jacksonville was a ghost town.

Still, people needed to eat. Under Eartha's supervision, a soup kitchen was opened at a black school, and meals were delivered to the bedridden. Other kitchens were opened and all told, 11,084 blacks and 5,709 whites were fed during this time. By the end of October, with 464 deaths in the city, the epidemic was declared over, and Eartha, along with the rest of Jacksonville, rejoiced.

On July 20, 1920, the forty-four-year partnership between Eartha and her mother ended with Clara's death. As profound as her loss was, Eartha paid tribute to her adored role model by officially revitalizing the Clara White Mission. With her own money and with contributions from friends, she moved the facility to larger quarters on Ashley Street, where it stands today, still the only nonprofit association dispensing daily meals to the poor in Jacksonville. It is also the source of another of Eartha's loving informal titles: "the Angel of Ashley Street."

As an active member of the Duval County Republican Party, she was an influential consultant to politicians who valued her opinion on a variety of racial issues. After women won the right to vote, Eartha urged black women to register and to vote despite threats from the Ku Klux Klan.

The breadth of Eartha's pursuits left little time for a social life. "I never married," she said. "I was too busy. What man would put up with me, running around the way I do?" Still, among letters she saved were love letters from one Albert Sammis, who lived in Tampa and who courted her for years by mail, apparently to no avail.

World War II galvanized her to take on a whole new round of patriotic activities related to services provided for area military personnel and their families by the Clara White Mission. Eartha also increased the hours and the scope of her Red Cross tasks, including organizing a baseball team to entertain the troops.

In 1955 a group of friends decided that as a woman in her seventies who had worked hard and unselfishly for others all her life, Eartha needed and deserved a rest. They surprised her with an all-expense-paid trip to Europe, which she accepted with gratitude and joy. That honor was one of many she received, including a Doctor of Laws degree from Edward Waters College and several other honorary degrees. Especially gratifying to Eartha was the realization of a lifelong dream with the dedication of the Eartha M. M. White Nursing Home in 1967, when she was ninety-one years old, and for which she actively solicited funds in the ninth decade of her life.

When she was ninety-four, she received the Lane Bryant Award for Volunteer Service. Asked how she would spend it, she replied, "I've already decided I want it to serve humanity. What would I do with it? Sit around the Plaza Hotel? I'm too busy." After the ceremony, she was the honored guest at President Nixon's reception in the White House, returning sometime later for a conference on aging.

A seemingly inexhaustible ninety-five-year-old, she received an appointment to the President's National Center for Volunteer Action, where she was seated to a standing ovation. She was also named Florida's outstanding senior citizen by Governor Askew in 1971, but to most who knew her, she was her state's outstanding citizen of whatever age group.

Her enormous, kind heart gave out and she died on January 18, 1971. She was buried in the city cemetery in Jacksonville, not surprisingly leaving all she had to charities. A 1971 *Floridian* article honored her, concluding: "She is, quite simply, an institution in Jacksonville. . . . She is a kind of universal mother to much of Jacksonville, particularly to the ghetto. She is the good earth."

Dr. Anna Darrow

1878–1959
DOC ANNER

Doctors Anna and Charles Roy Darrow had lived in Okeechobee only a short time before the night when there came a pounding on the door. Okeechobee was a tough, raw town. Nine-tenths of the white citizens were said to be on the run for one reason or another, and Dr. Roy refused to answer the door. Dr. Anna, who in her own words "didn't have sense enough to be scared," went to the window and called out, "Who's there?" The Darrows breathed more easily when Will Raulerson, a neighbor and upstanding citizen, answered, "Doc, my shoat is having convulsions." With her farm upbringing far in the past, Anna was unable to recall just what a shoat was. Thinking it might be a Cracker term for baby, she asked, "How old is the child?"

"Doc, it's my three–weeks–old pig that drank so much cane skimmings from the moonshine, he is having convulsions," came the answer.

She ran back to her husband. "His little piggy is drunk on cane skimmings from moonshine."

"What does he think I am, a vet?" Roy mumbled, pulling the covers closer.

Considering they had not yet established their reputations in Okeechobee, Anna opted for diplomacy and scurried back to the window, calling out, "How much does piggy weigh?"

"Twelve pounds" was the reply.

She hurried then to find her most prized possession—a kit containing a complete drug store, given to her at graduation by Dr. Abbott in Chicago. Extracting a chart from the kit, she made some quick mental calculations, poured some pills into a container, and wrote instructions on the label.

"What on earth did you prescribe?" her husband asked when she crawled back into bed.

"Abbott's combination for colic," she said.

It worked; piggy recovered. Doc Anna's reputation in Okeechobee was sealed but she couldn't help thinking it was a far cry from what she envisioned her life would be as Dr. Anna Darrow.

Anna Albertina Lindstedt was born on September 16, 1878, in Jasper County, Indiana, to Swedish immigrant parents of whom little is known except that they were hard-working farmers who evidently tired of so much hard physical labor, for they moved to Chicago when Anna was thirteen.

As a child, Anna had a talent for drawing, an appreciation for color, and a desire to preserve the beautiful things she saw around her. In Chicago schools, where she was taught art and drawing, she felt she was assuredly in her true element. She was thrilled to have two of her drawings exhibited in 1893 at the World's Columbian Exhibition, popularly known as the Chicago World's Fair. Hers were the only ones shown from the North Division high schools. She would mention them with pride during interviews more than fifty years later.

After graduation, she attended a business college where she met the young man who would become her husband, Charles Roy Darrow. They married and moved to Long Beach, California, where Roy assumed a position as assistant cashier in a bank. Dissatisfied, they migrated to Utah in 1900, where they opened a new and secondhand furniture store to supply railroad immigrants.

When a woman art teacher found herself unable to pay for furniture she had purchased, she offered to give Anna art lessons to settle the debt. The Darrows agreed and Anna progressed so rapidly, one of her paintings was valued at fifteen hundred dollars for insurance purposes.

Soon, Anna gave birth to a son, Richard. When he was three years old and she was pregnant again, Anna came down with a severe illness, at first thought by her Utah doctors to be grippe. But as her condition continued to worsen, they sent for Roy, who was away in Idaho selling furniture. By the time he arrived home, frightened and exhausted, she was improving, even though the doctors remained baffled as to a diagnosis.

She recovered, growing stronger as she and Roy both rested while commiserating on their inability to help each other and their frustration with local doctors. During the course of their conversations, they discovered something they hadn't known about each other. To their amazement, they both confided they had wanted to become doctors for a long time. By eleven o'clock that evening, they had agreed to enroll in Dr. Still's new college of osteopathy in Kirksville, Missouri, since they had furnished it and it was the only medical college they knew.

They closed the store in 1903 and Roy enrolled at once. Anna had to wait three weeks to deliver their new daughter, Dorothy. They both took summer work instead of vacations, allowing them to finish their courses in half the normal time. They then returned to Chicago to take night work at Jenner Medical College and the Chicago College of Medicine and Surgery, now known as Loyola University Medical School. The mother of two managed to graduate with honors in 1909.

Roy, who had never been in good health, was specializing in eye, ear, nose, and throat medicine when he contracted a severe case of the flu, which brought on heart disease. He was advised to seek a warmer climate. Louis Larson, a land agent for Florida's East Coast Railroad (ECR), was Roy's patient in Chicago. Through this contact, Roy secured the position of surgeon for the ECR. In 1909 the Darrow family arrived in Jacksonville, Florida, where mother and father promptly passed the Florida Board exams. Dr. Anna was just the second woman in the state's history to apply for a license, and she passed with "97+" written on her test.

James Ingraham, Henry Flagler's promoter and the vice president of ECR, convinced the Darrows to relocate to Okeechobee, assuring them that when the railroad got there, that small settlement was destined to become another Palm Beach or Miami. In 1911 the four Darrows bought a new "brass-bound, high-spoked wheel, Model T" and drove south on the Dixie Highway, hubcap-deep in water most of the way and with young Richard poised on the fender, pouring water into the open, steaming radiator.

Okeechobee, then known as Tantie and named for a red-headed schoolteacher, Tantie Huckabee, consisted of a scattering of ramshackle wooden buildings. The Darrows quickly built themselves a small house and opened an office. Since he was in frail health, Dr. Roy handled the office practice, which included pulling teeth and fitting glasses. Shortly, he built a two-story brick and concrete building to use as a drug store and office. After he secured the building materials, his Jacksonville bank failed and he lost all his money. There was nothing to do but borrow another five thousand dollars. The family lived on bacon and grits and Dr. Anna made all their clothes until the loan was repaid.

Physically stronger, Anna took the country practice, driving the Ford when she could and a horse and buggy when the car couldn't make it. Even a buggy couldn't make it to some patients, so then she rode a horse or rowed a boat. The horse, bought for a good price from a livery stable in Palm Beach, had been hit by a train, resulting in a peculiar gait that announced Dr. Anna's impending arrival to her patients.

Slim and pretty, she was also fearless, going alone wherever she was needed day or night, sometimes camping out for days in the buggy. She had a lantern wired to enable her horse to see the trail when nighttime travel was necessary. "If you never heard the roar of a bull alligator and some night bird answer, you haven't lived," she said. She never carried a gun and never had trouble with the rural people known as Crackers, who treated her with utmost respect.

She did begin to carry change for a hundred dollars after learning a favorite Cracker trick was to offer to pay her with a fifty-dollar bill. If she couldn't make change, her crafty patients considered the bill closed.

At first, her patients seemed ignorant to her, but she quickly learned their backwoods ways, gaining respect for their customs, although differences in speech could cause confusion. Once during a measles epidemic, she told a man she thought he was immune. He complained all over town to anyone who would listen, "Doc Anner thinks I'm a mule." Her compassionate nature manifested itself in small ways. She attended her patients' weddings and helped to lay them out for their funerals if that became necessary.

The Seminole Indians, whose nearest camps were thirty miles away, were understandably mistrustful of most whites, but they learned to have confidence in the "Squaw Doctor" who cared for them free of charge. They sometimes waited on her porch for days until she returned rather than see anyone else. They would give her gifts, such as a leg of venison or a whole turkey. She once came home to find ten Seminole women waiting for her with twenty-five quarts of huckleberries. Mostly, Seminole ailments consisted of malaria, hookworm, tonsillitis, and "Florida sores" caused by the sawlike teeth of the ubiquitous palmetto, which scratched wild hogs, carriers of lice and fleas. Men would be scratched by the same palmettos, resulting in ulcerating sores.

One time when she answered a middle-of-the-night call from the bedroom window, Anna was summoned by two men who said a woman needed her on a ridge where the Kissimmee River enters Lake Okeechobee. Despite not knowing the men, she dressed, drove her Model T to the dock, and boarded their small motorboat with them. They headed for the river in the mist-shrouded lake. After being stuck on a sandbar and searching desperately for a lantern that was to signal their destination, they finally spotted it and tied up at a rickety dock, several hours later.

Once onshore, they walked half a mile to a cabin where the men left Dr. Anna with a semiconscious woman. The woman awakened periodically with labor pains and was sweating profusely from a temperature of 106 degrees. Diagnosing malaria, Dr. Anna instituted treatment and delivered a baby girl at half past four in the morning. The baby cried a few times and then died. Placing it on a nearby trunk, Anna continued to care for the mother. Later, glancing back at the dead baby, she was horrified to see rats gnawing at the tiny corpse. Hastily wrapping it in a towel, she put it under a protective covering while she finished her work. Then, following instructions from the men who had returned, she went to eat breakfast at a house a quarter mile away. She was served by a woman whose only conversation was "Come in and set."

After breakfast, as she was cleaning up her patient, she became aware of a burning and itching all over her body. Upon investigating, she found fleas, hog lice, and some unnamed red bug on her skin. Quickly, she stripped, removed the insects, and dressed again, wondering as she did how she was to get home, since the men who had brought her there were nowhere to be seen and it was past noon. Almost immediately, another stranger appeared, led her to a boat, and started the return journey. There were no problems with visibility this time, but, due to a squall that had blown up, the small boat was tossed violently, nearly throwing her over the side several times and drenching both of them. Clutching her precious medical bag and hanging on, she was beginning to wonder if the whole business would ever end. Finally, they reached the mouth of the river. Never had she been so happy to see her reliable Ford at the riverbank.

Okeechobee, in those days, was a tough frontier town where catfishermen, cowboys, Crackers, African Americans, and Indians converged, not always peaceably. Saturday nights were routinely filled with scenes of drunkenness, fights, and shootings. Leland Rice, of the notorious Rice gang, went looking for trouble in the colored section of town one night and got half his jaw shot off. Bleeding, combative, delirious, and calling for his mother, he was taken by his gang to Doc Anner, as she was mostly called. She held his hand, pretending to be his mother, as she and Dr. Roy worked most of the night to stop the bleeding and patch up the outlaw enough to ship him to a hospital in St. Augustine. He recovered from that escapade but was not so lucky four months later when a sheriff shot him dead.

Another time when she was called to treat a woman in labor, she encountered a man who had been shot dead in front of the door with "his liver spattered around." She had to first push the body out of the way, so she could enter and deliver a baby, while "everyone but the mother" was hiding in the palmettos.

She treated men with tarantula bites, performed a curettage on a woman who was bleeding to death on a bouncing houseboat, and pumped out the stomach of a newly arrived doctor who had bragged that he was going to "run the petticoat doctor out of town." The last episode took place after the doctor, who also opened a drug store and who was fond of his liquor, picked up a tumbler that had been filled by a clerk with a poisonous liquid intended for another purpose, quaffed it, and collapsed.

As Okeechobee grew with the arrival of the railroad in 1915, there was much excited talk of expansion, perhaps even usurping Tallahassee's place as the state capital. Indeed, Dr. Anna seemed to have caught the bug, donating a tract of land for the new capitol. That never happened though, as Okeechobee was unable to recover after the post–World War I recession. In 1922 the Darrows, overworked and discouraged with the pace of things, pulled up stakes and moved to Stuart, Florida.

It was then that Anna became acquainted with members of the Ashley gang, a family of bank robbers and killers whose reign of terror on Florida's east coast lasted from 1911 until the last one was wiped out in 1924. Anna's acquaintance with the infamous outlaws began when John Ashley was in a Stuart jail, awaiting trial, and his mother, worried that he was not being treated properly, got a tonic for her son from Dr. Anna. The gang must have been satisfied with the treatment because on another occasion, they led her blindfolded ten miles into the woods to their hideout to treat another gang member, then out again, blindfolded once more, but by another trail to ensure secrecy.

The following summer the adventurous Anna and Roy toured the country as sales representatives for the Mosby Company, publisher of medical and dental books. They toured by car, carrying an oiled silk tent packed on the running board. Tourist camps were scarce and they often had to wait out a band concert or other event before retiring, because town parks were the only places they could find to stay.

They returned to Stuart in the midst of a boom, when no office space was available. A friend named Will Marshall, Fort Lauderdale's first mayor, told them his town needed doctors badly and offered them office space in his own building.

By this time, Richard and Dorothy had both graduated from Rollins College. Richard, who developed tuberculosis, went on to Arizona where he studied law. Dorothy continued her education at Columbia and would become Fort Lauderdale's librarian.

Anna and Roy decided the time was ripe to resettle again. They moved together to Fort Lauderdale in 1924, but just two short years later, the loving union ended with Roy's death, shortly after the 1926 hurricane. The forty-eight-year-old widow, with a lifetime of experiences already behind her, continued to practice medicine.

Her art had always been important, but she devoted more time to it after Roy's death and in 1947 won second prize, a bond worth one thousand dollars, in the Medical Art Exhibition sponsored by the Mead-Johnson Company during the American Medical Association convention. The year's theme was "Courage and Devotion Beyond the Call of Duty," a fitting description of the scene Anna had painted re-creating an incident she lived though in Okeechobee. It shows her exiting her Ford to walk a path to attend a patient, unaware that she's about to step on a coiled-up rattlesnake. She is saved by a mother hen flapping and charging at the snake to save her own brood of chicks as well as the approaching doctor. The patient's family is depicted standing on the porch, and a stork circles the sky with two babies in its beak.

Dr. Anna and her daughter both retired in 1949 and moved together to Coral Gables, where Anna continued to paint and garden. She suffered a cerebrovascular accident (stroke) in 1957 and another in 1959 when she died, one of Florida's toughest pioneers.

RUTH BRYAN OWEN

---◆◇◆---

1885–1954

FLORIDA'S FIRST CONGRESSWOMAN

Ruth Baird Bryan was five years old in 1890 when her father began his term as Nebraska's newly elected representative. The family joined him in Washington, D.C., and a fascination with politics took hold in the young child, growing within her and affecting her for the rest of her life.

The new congressman took his daughter to work, holding her small hand and encouraging her to be an eyewitness to the workings of the federal government. Sometimes she joined her mother in the gallery, riveted along with everyone else in the chamber by her father's spellbinding oratory. A religious man, longtime Democrat, and supporter of women's rights, William once noted, "political parties, like churches cannot long endure without participation of women."

She was eleven when she learned there could be glory in defeat. After her father's unsuccessful campaign for president in 1896, Ruthy and her mother accompanied him on a speaking trip to a small mining town nestled among towering mountains in Utah. Speaking from the balcony of the railroad station, her father concluded his stirring words by pledging to his audience that "all his life, whether in victory or defeat, he would fight the battles of the common people." The words deserved applause, but the audience of miners, all with lamps on their caps, was silent. Then, one after another, the men removed their caps, bowing their heads as though in church. After an eerie stillness, a trickle of applause began, escalating into a deafening roar that echoed throughout the valley.

Wide-eyed, Ruthy climbed into their carriage with her mother, watching the miners crowd forward, full of emotion, trying to shake

Ruth Bryan Owen   Florida State Archives

her father's hand or touch his coat. He had lost his election, but he won their hearts.

Ruth could hardly help but be affected, vowing on the spot to spend her own life in public service.

Ruth Baird Bryan was born on October 2, 1885, in Jacksonville, Illinois, the first child of William Jennings Bryan, a lawyer, three-time U.S. presidential candidate, and secretary of state under Woodrow Wilson, and his intelligent, educated wife, Mary Elizabeth (Mamie) Baird, who would also become a lawyer.

Ruth attended local public schools and then the Monticello Seminary in Godfrey, Illinois. She was a good student, precocious and exhibiting early evidence of superior intelligence. The scholar of the family, she cast off her dolls early on in favor of serious reading.

On an autumn visit in 1887 to a lawyer friend in Lincoln, Nebraska, William decided to join his friend's practice in that frontier town, temporarily moving there alone. Mamie remained behind to care for her father, who was blind, her mother, who was an invalid, and her baby daughter. By May 1888, after all details had been attended to, the family moved together into a fourteen-room house in Lincoln.

Mamie, an inspiring role model for her daughter, was almost casual in her account of those years. "After two and a half years of diligent work accomplished in addition to the care of my parents and my baby girl," she said, "I passed the examination and was admitted to the bar . . . being the only woman in the class and ranking third in a class of seventeen." She did not mention that at that time she was also pregnant again. Ruth's brother, William Jennings Bryan Jr., was born June 24, 1889. Her sister, Grace Dexter, arrived on February 17, 1891.

Beginning at age eight, Ruth showed some literary ability, writing stories with the encouragement of both parents. Her father liked to tell about the time he took her breakfast when she was in bed with measles. Sitting with her while she ate, he asked what she wanted to be when she was grown. "I'd like to write stories and books," she said, her eyes lighting up. Then, sadly, she added, "But I expect I'll get married and raise a family, like Mamma."

The family accompanied candidate Bryan on his campaign travels, covering over eighteen thousand miles in 1896 alone. Ruth helped her mother answer campaign mail and take care of other details such as figuring out what to do with some of the gifts the Bryans received from admirers—such as an enormous stuffed alligator, four eagles "of prodigious size and strength," as well as harnesses, suspenders, a mule, an ostrich egg, and a picture frame made of cigar boxes.

The trips provided an invaluable education for the young girl, even before she entered the University of Nebraska in 1901. In college, she joined the Delta Gamma sorority, participating in their activities, holding offices, and writing articles for their national magazine. She maintained her sorority ties for the rest of her life. They were the basis for the "old girl network" she used to her advantage later in her career.

To satisfy her ambition for public service, and with her parents' blessing, she left the university in 1903 to work at Jane Addams's Hull House in Chicago. Working at the settlement and helping immigrants gave her insight into the problems of youth and of the poor, which she would not forget.

When she was just eighteen, she married an artist, William Leavitt. She gave birth to a son and a daughter before the marriage ended in 1909. Left with no support for her children, she made her first venture onto the lecture platform under the auspices of the extension department of the State University of Nebraska. She also substituted for her father on the popular Chautauqua lecture circuit when he overbooked himself. It seemed only natural; it was in the family blood. Her speeches were well received and often she lectured every night for several months.

In the meantime, she frequently accompanied her now-famous father on many of his official travels during campaigns. Even after he lost in the 1896 presidential election, she remained interested, serving as his campaign secretary during his runs for president in 1900 and 1908. When her father was nominated in 1908, she was there cheering, before being escorted to the platform where she smiled, waving her scarf like a professional.

To provide a living for her children, she continued on the lecture circuit and wrote articles for a news syndicate, sometimes traveling to foreign destinations in that capacity. During one trip, she met Captain Reginald Altham Owen of the Royal Engineer Corps of the British Army. They married in 1910 and, by that act, Ruth lost her American citizenship according to a law in effect at the time. The couple traveled extensively in Europe and Jamaica. In 1913 they became parents of a son, Reginald Jr., nicknamed Bryan.

With the outbreak of World War I in 1914, Captain Owen was sent to Turkey, while Ruth remained in England with their son. She joined the American Women's War Relief Fund Association along with Lou (Mrs. Herbert) Hoover, Lady Astor, the Duchess of Marlborough, and other women, working for the Belgium food relief effort.

In her desire to be of service, she took a nursing course, joined the British Volunteer Aid Detachment, and worked as a nurse for three years in Egyptian war hospitals. It was an unhappy surprise when Reginald was admitted to her station, suffering from kidney disease. He insisted on returning to his unit after being treated and receiving a promotion to major. He developed scarlet fever in 1918 and was given ten years to live.

Hoping to benefit from the climate, the Owen family relocated to Coral Gables, Florida, near Ruth's parents, who had retired there three years previously. Ruth gave birth to daughter Helen Rudd in 1920, leaving her with a total of four children and a husband requiring her support. She turned again to a lecture tour, expanding her repertoire to include antiwar topics, which were important to women and which were an enduring interest for her for the remainder of her life.

In her own words, she joined every civic, church, or educational movement in Florida, including the Miami Women's Club, PTA, Theater Guild, DAR, Episcopal Church Guild, YMCA, League of Women Voters, League of American Pen Women, American Association of University Women, and more.

In 1925 she was employed in the speech department at the University of Miami. Because of her increasingly comfortable financial circumstances, she donated her teaching salary toward scholarships.

In an almost inevitable career move, she announced her candidacy for a Democratic seat in the U.S. House of Representatives in 1926, even though she was well aware that female candidates were not welcome in conservative Florida, nor in the rest of the South.

Contributing to her self-confidence was the award she received in 1927—an honorary Doctor of Laws degree from Rollins College. During the ceremony, the president of Rollins, Hamilton Holt, addressed her: "Good daughter of a good father, mistress of the spoken word, statesman of both achievement and promise, for your womanly service in the world crisis brought on by man's ignorance, obstinacy and folly, for your high concept of civic duty and for your many services to your state and nation, Rollins College bestows on you the degree of LL.D."

Then, the campaign began. She ran for the Fourth Congressional District, which encompassed a five-hundred-mile area from Jacksonville to Key West, and she ran against popular eleven-year incumbent and longtime Florida resident William Sears. Her marriage to an Englishman was brought up again and again as a reason to disqualify her. She engaged an attorney who attested to the fact that since she had lived in Florida seven years prior to the election, it was proper for her to run. She also paid for newspaper ads to inform the public that she had regained her citizenship in 1925 through naturalization procedures.

She lost the election by just 776 votes, which realistically was a triumph, considering the odds she had faced.

Another more tragic loss followed. Her husband died on December 12 of that same year. Defeated, grief-stricken, and suffering from severe depression, Ruth turned to her recently widowed mother and to her daughter Helen Rudd for strength. Remarkably, within two and a half months, she embarked on a second campaign for the U.S. Congress.

Some things hadn't changed: the politics of exclusion of women in Florida and her opponent, William Sears. What had changed was candidate Owen's more aggressive tactics.

To get around the huge district more efficiently, Ruth bought a sporty green Ford coupe and had "The Spirit of Florida, Ruth Bryan Owen's Car" prominently drawn on the rear spare tire cover. She began campaigning in every precinct of her district, drawing crowds wherever she went. She covered over sixteen thousand miles during the campaign, often making seven speeches a day, changing the tires on the coupe herself when necessary, and inspiring one editor to observe, "This weaker sex stuff is exploded for me forever."

Women especially were energized by her candidacy, forming supportive clubs all along Florida's east coast. She won the primary easily, in the largest voter turnout in history for the Democratic primary, according to the *Miami Herald.*

She then took some time off before the general election, again lecturing on the Chautauqua circuit to pay her bills.

While running against Republican William Lawson in 1928, Ruth promised to visit each county in her district every year, to get help for the victims of the two most recent calamitous hurricanes of 1926 and 1928, to support protective tariffs for Florida's farmers, and to sponsor two high school students to go to Washington every year to learn about their government.

On November 6, 1928, Ruth Bryan Owen became Florida's first congresswoman, carrying all but one county and losing that one by just 178 votes. She arrived in Washington, enthusiastically received by her male colleagues, except for one. Her vanquished opponent challenged the election, claiming by virtue of her 1910 marriage to a British citizen, she was no longer an American and could not hold public office. He declared himself the winner, quoting the Congressional Expatriation Act of 1907: "Any American woman who marries a foreigner shall take the nationality of her husband."

On January 17, 1930, Ruth defended herself before the House Committee on Elections without a lawyer, because, she said, the case was so simple, none was needed. She cited the Cable Act of 1922: "A woman citizen of the United States shall not cease to be a citizen of the United States by reason of her marriage after the passage of this act."

Asserting that her citizenship was questioned only because she was a woman, as never in history had a man lost his citizenship by marrying a foreigner, she movingly announced, "Never by word or act have I been anything but a loyal American citizen during my entire life. . . . You cannot deny my claim without saying to millions of American women that they are not entitled to the same treatment as men."

On March 1, 1930, the House Committee on Elections unanimously agreed with her and shortly after, the full House concurred.

Without further delay, Representative Owen took office and set to work, sponsoring two bills. One was to appropriate funds for the eradication of the Mediterranean fruit fly, which was capable of destroying Florida's prized fruit industry, and the other was to provide for flood disaster relief for farmers. She quickly involved herself in programs to safely develop rivers and harbors, becoming, according to another legislator, one of the most successful advocates of river and harbor legislation in Congress.

Mindful of her early statements that she was "going to Congress to represent the needs of an agricultural state," she voted for protective tariffs.

Backed by many women's groups who believed women had a right to independent citizenship, Representative Owen called for equitable application of the Cable Act, regardless of gender, citing defects in the wording of the original law. Her proposed amendments were signed into law by President Herbert Hoover in 1930.

An avowed conservationist, Ruth next sponsored a bill to create a national park within the Everglades. This was not solely her idea, but one she considered important enough to fight for, along with others, including Marjory Stoneman Douglas. Marjory related in her autobiography how, during the House committee debate, landowners who didn't want to sell land to the government for the park argued the Everglades was just a worthless swamp filled with snakes and mosquitoes. "To prove it," Marjory said, "they brought a big snake in a bag and dumped it on the table. Ruth Bryan Owen saw that something had to be done. She'd never picked up a snake in her life, but she grabbed this one, wrapped it around her neck and announced: 'That's how afraid we are of snakes in the Everglades.'" Less dramatically, Ruth also produced experts to back her bill. The House committee endorsed it, but the full House rejected it, fearful of committing such a huge sum of money during the Depression. It was disappointing, but at least it brought the idea to the attention of the public.

Another failed effort was her proposed cabinet-level Department of Home and Child, which she envisioned would "promote and foster education, home and family life, and child welfare." She devoted two years of hard work to the measure, but in the end, homes and children did not command other lawmakers' attention and the bill failed.

Although still enormously popular with her constituents and respected by other legislators, Ruth seriously miscalculated the public's wishes concerning Prohibition in her campaign of 1932. Having followed her father's temperate footsteps all her life, she stood for upholding the Eighteenth Amendment while her opponent, J. Mark Wilcox, sensed the turning of public opinion and boosted its repeal. Ruth lost the election but during her remaining time in Congress, although disappointed and exhausted, she scrupulously honored her commitment to represent the voters by voting to repeal Prohibition.

Just five months later, she became the first woman to represent the United States as head of a diplomatic legation when President Franklin Roosevelt appointed her minister to Denmark. Due to her popularity in the Senate, the appointment was unanimously approved without it being referred to the Foreign Affairs Committee as was customary.

She served well for three years, touring, speaking, and improving relations. She also fell in love again, this time with Captain Borge Rohde of the King's Life Guards. While he and Ruth were being married on July 11, 1936, in Hyde Park, New York, at President Roosevelt's church, some in Roosevelt's administration were resurrecting Ruth's old nemesis, marriage to a foreigner, fearing it might complicate things in Roosevelt's upcoming campaign. Even the staid *New York Times*, however, raised questions, noting that male diplomats had no such difficulties, but Ruth resigned rather than cause problems for the president.

During the next year, she traveled in a trailer across the country, promoting Roosevelt's reelection and writing books, including *Leaves from a Greenland Diary* (1935), *Denmark Caravan* (1936), *The Castle in the Silver Wood and Other Danish Fairy Tales* (1939), and *Picture Tales from Scandinavia* (1939).

She also worked to end wars by making speeches and writing anti-war articles, and when World War II broke out, she tried to help form an international peace organization. In 1943 she wrote *Look Forward Warrior*, in which she presented a peace plan for the nations of the world based on the principles of the United States government. It was widely praised, and, partly because of that book, President Truman appointed her special assistant to the San Francisco conference that formed the United Nations. Serving as alternate representative to the Fourth Session of the U.N. General Assembly in 1949, she continued speaking out and writing to promote peace.

During a trip to Denmark to receive the Danish Medal of Merit, she suffered a massive heart attack, dying in Copenhagen on July 26, 1954, at the age of sixty-eight. Her cremated remains were buried in the Ordrup Cemetery near Copenhagen. The Good Daughter had completed her service to others with integrity, dignity, and grace.

Rose Sayetta Weiss

1886–1974

MOTHER OF MIAMI BEACH

Traveling from New York City to Jacksonville, Florida, was a challenge in 1918. For an unaccompanied young woman who had never left Brooklyn since immigrating from Russia years before, attempting the trip with her two-year-old son could have been downright terrifying. Perhaps—for anyone but Rose Weiss, whose sunny disposition and sense of adventure made her almost forget the risks of such a trip.

Then, too, there was Rose's asthma. When the hazards of being the solitary caretaker of a toddler aboard a ship threatened to overwhelm Rose, she reminded herself that, like the pot of gold at the end of a rainbow, there was promised relief in Florida from the curse of her struggle to breathe.

Her doctors told her they had done all they could. Now, the only thing they could recommend was a move to a more healthful climate. A friend of hers who had moved to Miami Beach for similar reasons in 1918 wrote to Rose, urging her to try it. The climate had worked wonders for the friend.

Leaving the two older children with her husband, Rose took the baby and headed south to investigate. After disembarking at Jacksonville, they boarded a train for the last leg of their long journey. Some kindly Jewish women met them in Miami and guided them to a bus for the ride across the new County Causeway. Unhappily, the bus had a flat tire, nearly the last straw for the exhausted mother.

When they finally arrived at Brown's Hotel, Rose rented a tiny apartment with a kitchen and began treating herself to daily sunbaths in the gloriously golden, salty air.

Rose Sayetta Weiss   Florida State Archives

"I could breathe again," she said. "I fell in love with this place. It was paradise. Like living in Shangri-La, I was so happy."

Within three weeks, she was convinced she was "cured." She never wanted to leave. She was, at long last, home.

Rose Sayetta was born in Mezerich, Russia, in 1886, shortly before the violent anti-Semitic pogroms broke out in 1903. There was a previous period of persecutions from 1881 to 1884, but in the second pogrom, forty-five people were murdered and thirteen hundred homes and shops were plundered. This time, Rose's family, including her three sisters, Sadie, Bessie, and Stella, and brother, Jack, joined the heavy Jewish emigration to Europe and the United States. Rose's family, like many of the Jewish families that settled in urban centers, fled to the Lower East Side of New York, later settling in Brooklyn.

In time Rose married Jeremiah Weiss, a garment worker and native of the United States. The couple had three children, Milton, Malvina, and Eugene. An otherwise strong young woman, Rose suffered increasingly from the bouts of asthma that finally precipitated the move to Florida.

After sending for her husband and family, she bought an unfinished apartment house on Collins Avenue, borrowed fifty dollars to buy a stove, and began work on the building that would eventually emerge as the Royal Apartments.

After his arrival, Jeremiah found employment as a cutter in the manufacture of upscale ladies' clothing. Mothering three children kept her busy, but Rose still found time to explore. With her gregarious ways and quick wit, she soon was on friendly terms with the mayor, the police chief, and other pioneering families in the area, including an unrelated Weiss family. Joe Weiss was another asthmatic escapee from New York. In 1913 he opened a lunch counter that would ultimately become the world-famous Joe's Stone Crab Restaurant.

In 1920 the 7.1-square-mile island of Miami Beach was home to 644 year-round residents. Those were times of moonlight swims or beach parties when neighbors sang around bonfires and boys and men would fish from the jetties. Everyone splashed on oil of citronella; some even wrapped their legs in newspaper or armed themselves with a pine switch to ward off mosquitoes, and all considered themselves lucky to live on Miami Beach.

Rosie, as she was known to everyone, unknowingly began setting a record when she started attending city council meetings. Intensely interested in the business of her community, she never missed a city council meeting in thirty-eight years, a record unmatched by any council member, earning her the title of Miami Beach's "Unelected Eighth Councilman." She listened attentively, was not shy if a protest seemed necessary, and in time became a political force, without ever running for office. If political candidates passed her muster, she campaigned for them and they rarely lost their elections.

But first and foremost, Rosie was a mother to her own children and to anyone else in need. She joined the PTA at the only Miami Beach school and became an active participant. One day in 1920, while passing the elementary school at lunchtime, she noticed an unhappy-looking blond boy sitting in the doorway. When she asked why he wasn't in the lunchroom, he said he had lost his money, but she instinctively knew he was hiding something. She took him to the principal and arranged for the child to receive free lunches in exchange for doing small chores to make him feel he earned them. After school she took him for a haircut and cleaned him up. "I got some fresh clothes for him and took him home," she said. "When I rang the doorbell of his house and his mother came to the door, for a moment she didn't recognize her son. Then when she realized what I did, she started to kiss me."

Rose learned the family had come to Miami Beach for the husband's health, but he was out of work and they were sinking into poverty. Rose cajoled a hotel owner she knew to hire the mother and then pressured the city manager, who found employment for the father.

"Everyone helped me," she said. "They made it very easy for me to help others. From that day on it started. I saw to it no child did without lunch in our school, not if I knew about it."

Through the PTA, she became so interested in the local children, she started working with more of those in need and soon, on her own, was distributing clothes and food baskets at Thanksgiving and other holidays. Dismissing her own hard work, she said, "Everybody helped me and worked with me: the merchants, the hotel owners, the people who ran the city. They made it very easy for me to help others."

The city even donated money to help her help others, making her their "one woman welfare board," the Beach's first.

Word about her spread. "If you have trouble, go see Mrs. Weiss." She came to the aid of so many delinquent children, officials began to call her in the middle of the night to help youngsters in trouble.

While she was "welfaring," as she called it, she organized a bazaar to raise funds for a library, helped plant trees on the new causeway, and sold doughnuts on the bridge for the Salvation Army. She was instrumental in setting up a prizefight to fund a city hospital, hiring the fighters herself and selling hundreds of tickets.

From its earliest years, Miami Beach was a magnet for colorful characters, including Pete Chase, owner of a defunct molasses factory in Key West. In 1921 he decided to start a chamber of commerce in Miami Beach, an idea ridiculed by many of the town's seven hundred citizens. Rosie, by then the proud owner of the fifteen-unit Royal Apartments, was among the first to join. She personally enrolled sixty members, earning the title of Membership Chairman and, later, an honorary life membership. During 1921 and 1922 the chamber consisted of a beach umbrella and bunting-draped table at the end of the causeway, but the three hundred members made it a real force on the Beach.

Chase went on to become a sales manager and a friend of Carl Fisher, Miami Beach's flamboyant developer. Meeting through Chase,

Rosie and Fisher became friends. Fisher honored her by choosing her to ride his elephant, "Rosie," as a publicity stunt for a tree-planting ceremony on the new County Causeway. Years later, near the end of his life, Fisher would tell her, "I built Miami Beach with my money, Rosie—but you built it with your spirit."

During Florida's boom years, from 1923 to 1926, the air crackled with excitement. Buildings were under construction everywhere and people poured into the area—ordinary tourists, celebrities, gamblers, and less desirables, including Al Capone, Public Enemy Number One.

After four years in her Shangri-La, Rose had made enough money on her apartments to join a partnership buying a block of business buildings in Fort Lauderdale that included a bank, post office, stores, and offices, all rented. When profits reached seventy-five thousand dollars, she begged her fellow investors to sell. They condescendingly calmed her feminine fears, and she bowed to their manly business judgment, but quietly kept her Royal Apartments safely separate.

By 1925 the Miami Beach population had increased to 2,342 persons, including more Jewish immigrants from the eastern seaboard.

As she strolled down Collins Avenue one day, Rosie spotted a sign on a piece of property reading "For Gentiles Only." The young woman who had fled the Russian pogroms, the pioneer who had done so much for her adopted community, paused momentarily and then did what she always did. She rolled up her sleeves and set to work to help make things right.

"I tried to do the right thing and to educate the Gentile people a little bit what a Jewish woman is like and believe me it helped," she said later. She ceaselessly strove to reduce anti-Semitism by demonstrating that Jewish people are worthy and equal and by selflessly working for deserving causes. With her engaging personality and movie-star smile, she was an awesome ambassador for her people. She was proud of her work in this area, considering it the most important contribution of her lifetime.

St. Francis Hospital, which she helped to found and then volunteered at when it was the only hospital on the Beach, was another cause to which Rose devoted countless hours. When Mt. Sinai Hospital was established, she volunteered there, too, and was a founder of the Douglas Gardens Home for the Elderly, which would become a state-of-the-art facility on a twenty-acre campus.

In 1926 signs indicated the Florida boom was over. New construction continued over the hot, sluggish summer, but on September 17 Mother Nature added her own brand of excitement with a brisk morning wind that strengthened throughout the day. News of a hurricane having passed Puerto Rico two days before was posted by the weather bureau. By afternoon, walking on Collins Avenue was made nearly impossible by gusts of stinging sand. By ten o'clock, rising tides caused water to seep under the doors at the Royal Apartments, and Rose was concerned about her tenants, especially one woman with a premature baby. She installed mother and baby on top of a lobby table. She had her son bring a frightened invalid and his wife from the building next door as the weather bureau began telephoning people all over the Beach, their only means of giving warning.

Winds of 125 miles per hour screamed all night, drowning the sounds of the collapsing of half-finished buildings, roofs ripping from houses, and boats crashing into homes.

The sudden silence at six o'clock the next morning fooled many people, but longtime Miami Beach residents knew the winds would resume and tried to warn newer residents not to leave their homes to survey the damage. Within a half hour, scores of people were caught in the raging wind roaring from the other direction, and by nightfall 113 people were dead. The Florida boom was a distant memory.

Rosie was one of the first out the next morning, surveying her community. Happy to be alive, happy her family and tenants were safe, and happy to see the sun shine, she inched her way through the muck and debris toward city hall to find out what needed to be done. On the way, she met a merchant who had lost everything. He responded to her sunny greeting by asking in surly Yiddish if she would be going back to Brooklyn. She indignantly dismissed the idea, giving him a piece of her mind before continuing on to Carl Fisher's office, where Pete Chase and others were sitting morosely, resembling nothing so much as morticians.

"Oh, excuse me," Rosie said. "I thought I came to Fisher's office—I see I came to a morgue." They had to laugh as she continued her pep talk.

When word got around about her lecture to the Jewish merchant, she was asked to repeat it at the next chamber of commerce meeting and she did.

Referring to her beloved Miami Beach, she said, "I'll love it when it'll be cleaned up more than ever before. As long as I own a grain of sand, I'll stand on it and help fix up this Miami Beach." The succeeding applause was deafening.

They were not empty words. Rosie worked tirelessly with the Red Cross to get milk and other supplies to stranded citizens, according special attention to overlooked African-American shantytowns. Her home became a Red Cross emergency station, and she led an effort to get bottled gas to the Beach for use in cooking. Children were always her first priority, and when planes flew over, dropping their cargo of milk, she personally saw to its delivery.

When the emergency abated, the Red Cross asked people who had assisted them during the crisis to submit bills for their expenses. When none was forthcoming from the Mother of Miami Beach, she was asked for one.

"I don't give bills for helping others," she said.

"Just for your expenses," they said. "Your car, gas, etc."

"I don't want it. I don't need it." And that was the end of that.

When Palm Beach was hit with another hurricane in 1928, Rosie, the expert, collected clothes and two thousand dollars for the stricken neighboring area.

By this time, she was so well known, mail addressed to "Rosie, Miami Beach" never failed to reach her. A member of Hadassah, the Women's Auxiliary of the American Jewish Congress, and the B'nai B'rith, she also chaired the committee to install Miami Beach's first community Christmas tree.

Before the crash of 1929, Rosie had borrowed to meet the mortgage on her Fort Lauderdale investment. When her bank failed, along with many others, she lost it all.

A natural optimist, she refused to dwell on her losses, focusing instead on her proudest achievements—her children. There was Milton, who became president of Miami Beach Federal Savings and Loan Association and of the Greater Miami Jewish Federation. Malvina, an educator, would become director of elementary education for Greater Miami, an adviser to President Dwight Eisenhower, and a member of the faculty at the University of Miami. Eugene, a podiatrist practicing in Miami Beach, became president of the Florida Podiatry Association.

As a member of the Miami Beach and Dade County Democratic Party, Rose was invited to sit with guests on the podium in Miami's Bayfront Park when Franklin Roosevelt came to town for a pre-election rally in 1932. Fortunately, she was hungry and told her companions to go on ahead, and she would meet them after she stopped for a hot dog. As a result, her chair was occupied by the unfortunate mayor of Chicago, Anton Cermak, who was struck and mortally wounded by an assassin's bullet intended for FDR. Rosie was saved by a hot dog.

In 1940 the Beach had twenty-eight thousand year-round residents, increasing to seventy-five thousand in the winter season. There were 239 hotels and 706 apartment houses. One six-unit house belonged to

Rose, who, in her usual fashion, had bounced back from difficult financial times and was doing nicely.

That year, German U-boats slipped into the Florida Straits, looking for merchant ships in the Gulf Stream, just forty miles from shore. For eighteen months, Florida's eastern beaches were littered with oil-soaked debris and even some bodies, from ships that burned within sight of land. Those chilling scenes, combined with government-ordered blackouts and fuel shortages, effectively killed tourism in southern Florida. Seasonal buildings would have been empty but for the thousands of servicemen and their families stationed on the Beach.

Since one-fourth of all Army Air Force officers and one-fifth of the enlisted men trained at Miami Beach, housing was at a premium. Soldiers with families had difficulty renting because of inflated rents and many landlords' refusals to rent to people with children.

Proud to be an American, Rosie posted a sign on her Royal Apartments: "Renting Only to Soldiers with Children" and cut the rent 20 percent for servicemen. A newspaper story, complete with a picture of Rosie surrounded by children, soon caused others to follow her example.

She also sold over five million dollars' worth of savings bonds, the largest amount of any woman in Florida. When the Mother of Miami Beach heard about an ailing, homesick soldier who had no relatives nearby, she promptly cooked him some Jewish penicillin (chicken soup) and nursed him back to health.

After the war, Rosie designed Miami Beach's official flag, using a gold background to represent sand, a green palm tree, and a blue sky. It was presented to the city and formally adopted on April 5, 1950. It remains the official flag except for the blue having been changed to green.

The long marriage of Rose and Jeremiah ended with his death in 1957, but even that couldn't slow Rosie down.

After attending a program celebrating Miami Beach's fiftieth birthday, she acted as the city's mother again, scolding the city council for leaving early pioneers out of the celebration. She was in her eighties and had missed some council meetings by that time, but she gave notice she would resume her old habit of attending them all.

Despite her busy life, she was experiencing some aches and pains. Eugene's wife, Ruth, took her for a checkup, and the young doctor who was filling in for her regular physician, prodded, probed, and listened to her complaints. Then, not very sympathetically, he reminded her of her age and informed her she must expect such discomforts if she was going to continue her active lifestyle. "Are you finished?" she asked. When he nodded, she offered her not very favorable opinion of his attitude and added she hadn't come for a lecture. "If I wanted that," she said, "I'd have gone to the University of Miami."

As her frailties increased, Eugene and Ruth pleaded with her to live with them, but Rosie had other ideas.

"I helped to found Douglas Gardens," she said. "That's where I'll live." And, feisty as ever, she had her way. Asked at age eighty-seven what in her life she would like to change, she said, "Nothing. I haven't got any diamonds or furs, but I've got my memories. And oh, what memories they are."

Rose died on August 6, 1974, and was buried in Mount Sinai Cemetery, her debt to America paid in full.

MARJORY STONEMAN DOUGLAS

1890–1998

MOTHER OF THE EVERGLADES

In the sweltering high school gymnasium of Everglades City, the speakers and the audience took turns slapping and scratching at the mosquitoes swarming through the open windows. When a frail elderly woman wobbled to the microphone, determined to convince the Dade County Commission that a strip of the Everglades needed to be zoned to prevent development, the hubbub swelled with boos and catcalls from landowners and developers, rendering useless any attempt on her part to speak. They knew who she was.

Among the more kindly suggestions shouted from the audience were hints that she should return to Russia, presumably the land of her birth.

Half the size of the other speakers, the woman calmly peered down through enormous tinted glasses, stoically biding time beneath her trademark floppy hat until some civility prevailed, at which time she sweetly announced, "That's all right. Carry on. I can stay here all night."

Then, as she had most of her life, Marjory Stoneman Douglas said what needed to be said, in her no-nonsense style, tempered with a touch of humor. By the end of the evening, zoning had passed to prevent development in at least one part of the Everglades, remarkably, since the gathering took place in the 1970s, when saving the Everglades was far from a popular cause and Marjory Stoneman Douglas was in her eighties.

Rarely, if ever, in her long life had she feared saying honestly what was on her mind. Describing her childhood self in her autobiography, *Marjory Stoneman Douglas: Voice of the River,* she noted that she had a crooked nose and a crossed left eye, was fat and unattractive, and her

Marjory Stoneman Douglas in April 1985   Florida State Archives

appearance was topped off with stringy, mouse-colored hair. Another time she observed it was better to be plain and unnoticeable. "You get by with a lot more," she said. "I can speak from experience about that."

Marjory was born in Minneapolis in 1890 to a musical mother, Lillian Trefethen, and Frank Stoneman, a man whose constant schemes to make a fortune consistently failed. Not realizing how much Lillian had been affected by one particularly disastrous business venture, Frank moved the family to Rhode Island, determined to make a new start.

When Lillian promptly suffered the first of several nervous breakdowns, the extended family, blaming the husband, installed Marjory's mother in a sanitarium and hauled Marjory off to Massachusetts to be raised by her grandmother and a doting Aunt Fanny.

Marjory read her way through her childhood, disdaining dolls in favor of books. It didn't matter what kind of books, she later recalled, she would read the encyclopedia if nothing else was available. Grandma's bookcase was a gold mine, holding Dickens, Shakespeare, Byron's poems, and history books, which she read and reread so that by the time she was in first grade, she was already reading in the back of her schoolbooks while her classmates dawdled at the front. Of the many kinds of lessons Grandma provided, Marjory's favorite was elocution, which she "took to like a duck to water," she said, crediting her lifelong ease in speechmaking to those early instructions. "I could talk to five hundred people as well as to two people even as a child," she said.

In spite of family financial trouble, Marjory attended nearby Wellesley, majoring in English Composition. The first class assignment was to write a letter home. Impressed by the colorful fall leaves on campus, Marjory's paper rhapsodized about their beauty. Her teacher had her read the letter out loud in class as an example of what not to write, but she got a round of applause from her classmates anyway, establishing her reputation as a writer for the rest of her campus career.

She excelled in the class she cared most about—English—and did poorly in that which did not interest her—trigonometry. Candidly, she admitted to being dateless for four years due to the fact that she was "unattractive, overweight and had a nervous giggle."

An enthusiastic member of the recently formed Suffrage Club at Wellesley, she was convinced she should have the right to vote and to use her valuable education that was teaching her to think and reason.

Following graduation and her mother's death from breast cancer, Marjory began a brief and disastrous marriage to a newspaperman thirty years her senior, who turned out to be a check forger and heavy drinker.

"I didn't regret my marriage, and I didn't regret leaving it, either," she said. "It was an education but now it was over . . ."

She headed south to Miami to become reacquainted with her father and await the finalization of her divorce. Her father had sent her money for the trip, inviting her to move in with him and his second wife, Lilla, who welcomed Marjory with open arms. Lilla would become and remain Marjory's best friend in Florida.

Marjory was relieved to be free of the pressures of her disastrous marriage and excited at the prospect of renewing ties with the father she had last seen when she was six years old. She learned he had passed the bar and practiced law for ten years before acquiring an old flatbed press as payment for a bad debt, and with it, he had started up Miami's first morning newspaper, the *News Record,* which would later become the *Miami Herald.* Marjory gratefully accepted a job as the society reporter, eager to begin her new life doing what she loved. She didn't care what she was writing as long as she was writing. Besides, she said, "any idiot ought to be able to write for a newspaper."

As she learned her way around Miami, then a city of less than five thousand people, Marjory was also learning the newspaper business from her father who treated her as he did any of his other reporters, particularly in demanding strictly accurate facts. "I sent you out to do a story and you come back with three sunsets and an editorial," he once complained when she waxed poetic in the early days. He made no distinction between women's and men's intellect or salaries and was delighted to discover he and Marjory had similar minds. Both were bookworms who enjoyed arguing endlessly about their favorite authors.

In her capacity as the society reporter and then as a columnist, Marjory observed the spirited women of Miami organizing fashion shows among the palm trees. Nearly two hundred women formed a Women's Club, spending their afternoons holding concerts, reading in their small library, the only one in town, or meeting to discuss books, politics, or news events. They were mostly content to let their husbands conduct the city's business, but they wanted to be informed.

Through her job, the young reporter met politicians and visiting celebrities, including Clarence Darrow and Mr. and Mrs. William Jennings Bryan. After his retirement as secretary of state, Mr. Bryan and his wife built a beautiful mansion in Miami, and Marjory was sometimes invited to visit.

Mrs. Bryan and Marjory shared an interest in women's suffrage, not a popular cause in Florida. In 1916 the women were joined by May Mann Jennings and Annie Broward, both wives of former governors, and Ivy Stranahan of Fort Lauderdale on a trip to Tallahassee to lobby the legislature for suffrage. Having prepared carefully and dressed meticulously, the women presented their case to committee members who sat in two lines with their backs propped against the walls, spittoons between them.

"No one said a thing," Marjory said. "They all sat there and spit into spittoons. Ping! They acted as if we weren't there at all." During a subsequent speech, Marjory recalled, "I never saw such an array of blank faces. We could have been talking to a bunch of dead mackerel, for all the response we got." Florida would be the last state in the union to ratify the suffrage amendment.

With World War I raging in Europe, the Navy sent a ship to Miami to enlist people in the Naval Reserve. Assigned to do a story on the first woman to join from Florida, Marjory let her enthusiasm get the better of her and enlisted herself. The U.S. Navy saw fit to employ her at its reserve headquarters at the foot of Flagler Street. She did office work and handed out boat licenses. It was, she said, the most wasted year of her life. Upon her honorable discharge a year later, she declared the day was probably "as great a break for the Navy as the invention of the carrier."

After her stint in the Navy, she spent time overseas with the Red Cross, but the pull of her adopted state was strong, and in 1920 she returned to the *Herald* as an assistant editor and columnist. Surviving two failed love affairs, she began to realize she was not the marrying kind. More than anything, she wanted her own life, and she wanted writing to be a big part of it.

Her father's support for a tiny committee working for the establishment of an Everglades National Park ignited Marjory's interest in the cause that would one day consume her. The survival of the Everglades was not the only progressive idea she inherited from her father. In filling the role of part-time magistrate during his early years in Miami, Mr. Stoneman earned a reputation for unconditional fairness between the races. Marjory detested the plight of blacks in Florida, a throwback to conditions in the Old South. In her autobiography, she said, "To me, slavery was the greatest crime ever committed, which we are still suffering to expiate." At her father's suggestion, she started a Baby Milk Fund at the *Herald* to raise funds to provide milk for needy babies. It was the first non–church-sponsored charity in Miami.

The daily stresses of writing her own column, investigating, and reporting began to take a toll on Marjory, leading to nervous fatigue. In 1924, with the understanding of her father, she left her position at the *Herald* to launch a new career as a freelance writer. It was the beginning of a long, informal association with the *Saturday Evening Post,* the leading magazine of the time. Her later fame as an environmentalist tended to overshadow her literary accomplishments: plays, books, short stories, and poems, of which she was justifiably proud.

Her new life suited her. For a loner, it was the perfect job. She worked when she wished, for herself, without a boss. She continued her freelance career until the early 1940s.

Meanwhile, the young career woman needed a home of her own. She purchased a lot in Coconut Grove that was surrounded by friends' homes, and in 1926 the place she would call home for the rest of her life was built. It was simple—one great workroom with living quarters attached. Although there was room for her growing book collection, there was no room for a stove, a minor detail since she didn't intend to cook much and a hot plate suited her just fine. There was no driveway either, as she never learned to drive and didn't own a car. Her funny little house withstood the great hurricane of 1926 with just $250 in damage.

The death of her Aunt Fanny, followed closely by that of her beloved father, plus a significant loss of eyesight, left Marjory heavyhearted but with a small inheritance that enabled her to live and begin work on a novel. That project was short-lived, however, when an old friend who was editing a series called "Rivers of America" asked her to write a book for the series. That book eventually became *The Everglades: River of Grass*, the work that changed the way the country perceived the Everglades.

"There are no other Everglades in the world." Its first sentence dares us to not pay attention. The book has never been out of print since it was published in 1947, and its first printing sold out in a month. The book's publication coincided with the founding of Everglades National Park, a project that came to fruition after a twenty-five-year struggle. As a long-time member of the committee formed to bring about the establishment of the park, Marjory was honored to be invited to the 1947 dedication ceremony, attended by President Harry Truman and other notables.

Marjory's next years were satisfying ones, filled with good times with friends, some travel, and writing books that were mostly successful, although not so much as *River of Grass*. That book was twenty years old and Marjory was seventy-eight when she founded the organization called the Friends of the Everglades, beginning a whole new career of lobbying, speechmaking, charming, and haranguing, all in the name of Florida's wild places and beings. "It's women's business to be interested in the environment," she said, eyes twinkling through her dark, thick glasses. "It's an extended form of housekeeping, isn't it?"

Launching the Friends of the Everglades was one of those unexpected occurrences that seemed to happen in Marjory's life. Always interested in anything concerning the Everglades, she had been closely following two bizarre proposals by developers, one to build a jet port in the Glades, another to build an oil refinery in Biscayne Bay. A casual compliment in a grocery store to an Audubon Society worker on the good work they were doing resulted in a challenge to get involved herself. Then, when she offhandedly asked another acquaintance his opinion as to whether an organization called Friends of the Everglades should be started and if enough people would join for one dollar, he enthusiastically supported the idea, handing her a dollar bill. She had a dues-paying member and a name and she was stuck.

The more she learned about the Everglades, the more determined she was to spread the word about the importance of the area, concentrating not only on developers but also on the Army Corps of Engineers and the Central and Southern Flood Control District. Both organizations were intent on draining water off the land to please farmers, sugar cane growers, and cattle ranchers. There were peat fires every spring on the drained land, and manure from the area ended up in the rivers flowing into Lake Okeechobee, turning the lake ugly brown. The artificially straightened Kissimmee River provided less water to the lake, which had less water for the Everglades, which had less water to evaporate into rain. Since evaporation of rain water, followed by rain storms, was the sole source of drinking water for over five million people in south Florida, it was imperative to do something besides fund another study in a long line of studies.

Her childhood elocution lessons again proved invaluable. Marjory made speeches about the Everglades anywhere, anytime, to a group of two hundred citizens or a legislative committee of two. As more people became interested in the cause, she took her cue from the friend who recruited her, challenging people to get involved. No one escaped her unshakable tenacity—developer, politician, sugar farmer, cattle rancher.

"I know I've got my enemies," she said. "The developers don't like me. The farmers don't like me. But I'm a dedicated environmentalist, and I want everyone to become aware of what is going on because that's the only way we'll stop all this terrible destruction. People need to realize that this is all there is. We don't have a limitless supply of everything."

U.S. Senator Bob Graham remembered that when he was a Florida state legislator, he was informed by Marjory that the legislature should safeguard the health of the Everglades and if they didn't "they would all spend an uncomfortable afterlife in hell." He and Marjory became good friends, but it was a friendship Marjory never minded using for the advantage of the environment. When Graham became governor of Florida, he started a program to restore the Kissimmee River, against the advice of engineers but with Marjory's delighted approval.

She never hesitated to take advantage of the sympathy evoked by her advanced age and frailties to badger people to make them understand why the Everglades were important to the future and economy of Florida. "The Everglades is a test," she said often. "If we pass, we get to keep the planet."

Bowing slightly to her lessening physical powers and loss of eyesight and hearing, Marjory relied more and more on good friends, old and new, to enable her to get about her business. When she lectured on Florida history at Dade Community College, she befriended a male student who volunteered to be her driver, eventually guiding her around Paris when she was eighty-seven years old. Personal secretaries wrote for her and read to her six days a week. She enjoyed the arrival of her housekeepers and their departure. "I've never been lonely," she said, "just alone. I think people who can't stand being alone are silly. How do they know who they are or what they're like if they're never alone?"

Awards and honors accumulated along with invitations to speak. Named for her are a manatee, a small park in Coconut Grove, schools in Miami-Dade and Broward Counties, and a government building in Tallahassee. After the Marjory Stoneman Douglas Everglades Protection

Act was amended to delay penalties for polluters, she ordered her name removed from the law. It was.

A 1.3-million-acre wilderness area in the Everglades was dedicated in her name on the fiftieth anniversary of Everglades National Park. Friends said she was most touched by that honor.

She personally cut the ribbon at the dedication ceremony for a high school named for her on her 100th birthday; received from President Clinton the Presidential Medal of Freedom, the highest civilian honor, on her 103rd birthday; and graciously accepted a Wonder Woman birthday cake from schoolchildren on her 105th birthday. Yet when someone would praise her for "saving the Everglades," she would quickly correct them: "It's not saved yet."

On May 14, 1998, at age 108, Marjory died at her old home in Coconut Grove, leaving instructions for her ashes to be spread in her cherished Everglades and for a service to be held in the park.

Marjory was one of the nineteen women inductees into the National Women's Hall of Fame at Seneca Falls, New York, for the year 2000. The Voice of the River is silent but her legacy lives on.

ZORA NEALE HURSTON

1891–1960
A GENIUS OF THE SOUTH

When Mama called nine-year-old Zora to her bedside to tell her what to do when Death entered the room, Zora promised to obey her mother's wishes. Rejecting local superstitions, Mama did not want the pillow taken from under her head until she was dead. The clocks and the looking glass were not to be covered as folklore said they must be to avoid bringing doom upon the home.

"Promise me," Mama said.

It was an easy promise to make. Mama was sick, but she could not die.

But later that day, as the sun began to set, Mama's spirit seemed to follow. Coming in from play, Zora watched the neighbor women help her father turn Mama's bed to face east, so it would not be crossways to the world, and in that terrible moment, she understood. Mindful of her promise, she struggled against the women and fought the strong arms of her father, battling the customs of centuries to honor her mama's wishes.

"She doesn't want that," Zora cried. "Don't take the pillow from under her head!"

Ignoring her screams, they covered the clock and the looking glass. Zora thought she felt her own heart break as her mother looked at her, trying to speak.

Ever after, Zora would, at times, agonize, wondering if her mother had been trying to remind her of the promise, if Mama believed in the last moments of her life that her daughter had failed her.

Zora Neale Hurston's carefree childhood was over.

Her life had begun, according to her autobiography, in 1901. Her birth certificate has never been found, but she also claimed she was born in 1903 and in 1910. According to the recently discovered family Bible of her parents, Lula and John Hurston, Zora was born in 1891. The Bible, now in the possession of Zora's niece, also confirms a long-held rumor that Zora was born in tiny Notasulga, Alabama, not in Eatonville, Florida, as she claimed all her life, perhaps wishing it were true.

Eatonville, just north of Orlando, the first all-black community in America, was where the Hurston family moved before Zora was two. Her mother was a seamstress and her father was a carpenter, sometime Baptist preacher, and mayor of Eatonville from 1912 to 1916.

Zora had one sister and six brothers, one brother having died in infancy. They lived in a big house with enough ground for a five-acre garden and plenty of room for neighborhood children to join them in play. Oranges, grapefruit, tangerines, and guavas grew in their yard for picking or throwing at each other, if the need arose. Outside by the chinaberry trees, they snacked on boiled eggs from their chickens, occasionally using those, too, for children's warfare.

Zora, a high-spirited child, was called arrogant and impudent by some, including her father and grandmother, but was defended by her mother who encouraged all her children to "jump at de sun." Every night after supper, games of "hide and whoop" and "chick-mah-chick" gave way to the serious business of homework. None of the children were excused until Mama was convinced they knew their lessons for the following day. Her perseverance produced outstanding adult citizens. One of Zora's brothers became a physician, one a pharmacist, another a high school principal, another owned a successful meat market in Jacksonville, one was a postman in New York City, and another became a chef. Sister Sarah would marry in haste and struggle with a no-good husband who was "wished a short sickness and a quick funeral" by the siblings.

Zora couldn't remember when she began telling the "lying tales" that so nettled her grandmother, only that it came as natural as breathing. Miss Corn Shuck began her adventures one day as Mama cooked roasting ears. She was joined in matrimony to Mr. Sweet Smell, a cake of soap from Mama's dresser drawer, by the Reverend Door Knob, who had fallen off the kitchen door. Zora entertained playmates with tales about the exploits of a local resident who lived on the outskirts of town and turned into an alligator at night. Her best audience was Mama, even when Zora told about the bird that talked to her from its perch on top of a tree and that had a tail so long it touched the ground. Even when Zora told how she had walked on top of the lake and watched the fishes swim under her feet, Mama listened.

Then came the monstrous, cruel day when Zora believed she failed her dying mama. "It seemed," she said in her autobiography, "as she died that the sun went down on purpose to flee away from me."

In less than a year, her father took a new bride, twenty-year-old Mattie Moge, whose hatred for Zora was reciprocated in full and then some. When Mattie tried to discipline Zora for her "sassy, impudent" ways, a vicious fight erupted.

By her own description in her autobiography, *Dust Tracks on a Road*, Zora said: "I wanted her blood and plenty of it. . . . Maybe she did not have the guts, and certainly she underestimated mine. . . . She scratched and clawed at me, but I felt nothing at all. . . . I could see her face when she realized that I meant to kill her."

The violence ended only by the physical intervention of her father.

Banished from home, Zora claimed she was "a slave ship in shoes" for the next seven years, shuffling from relative to relative, to boarding school and back, experiencing the first unhappy period in her life.

When her older brother Bob, who was by then a busy doctor with a wife and three children, sent for her to come and live with them in

Memphis, Zora's joy was indescribable. "I was going to have a home again. I was going to school. I was going to be with my brother!"

What seemed too good to be true was. No school for a while was the plan, Bob told her. She was needed around the house to help her sister-in-law. If she would be patient, things would work out. The irrepressible Zora chafed under her new restrictions and the hard work expected of her. When an opportunity arose to work as a lady's maid for an actress, Zora jumped at it.

The young actress and Zora hit it off from the start. Not only did Zora have more money than she ever had in her life, she was thrilled by the backstage life, enjoying the joking and camaraderie among the show people as she became educated about food, clothes, and life's finer things. Within the year, when her employer prepared to leave the stage for marriage, she arranged for Zora to finish high school, at age twenty-six, and to begin classes at Howard University in Baltimore.

Zora fell in love with college life and with fellow student Herbert Sheen, who was hoping to become a doctor. She was pleased with her studies and teachers and with being accepted into the prestigious Stylus literary club. Always pinching pennies, she helped herself financially by working as a manicurist, a trade the actress had wisely insisted she learn while working backstage. Making friends was always easy for Zora and now, through friends, she was able to find a job as a waitress at the swank Cosmos Club and as a maid for prominent black Washington families.

Her literary talent quickly became apparent at Howard, where before long, she received a scholarship to Barnard in New York City. She quickly transferred there. Following a chance meeting, the novelist Fanny Hurst hired Zora as a live-in secretary despite Zora's poor typing skills. Impressed with Zora's "blazing zest for life," Hurst provided Zora with living quarters in her home. Influenced by Barnard's intellectual pioneers in the field of anthropology, Zora switched her studies from English to anthropology, concentrating particularly on folklore.

The 1920s were the days and nights of the Harlem Renaissance, when white people flocked to clubs and parties in Harlem. Zora did not drink, but she was part of the scene, dressing as glamorously as she could afford, smoking in public, and enjoying being the life of the party. Her friend, writer Langston Hughes, said she was "full of side-splitting anecdotes, humorous tales, and tragi-comic stories, remembered out of her life in the South. . . . To many of her friends, no doubt, she was a perfect 'darkie,'—that is a naïve, childlike, sweet, humorous and highly colored Negro." But she was always Zora, never hiding her roots, even when she met white publishers, show people, or Wall Street executives. She was Zora from all-black Eatonville and, as the famous writer Alice Walker would say many years later, "She was outrageous—it appears, by nature."

Of all the young black writers of the Harlem Renaissance era, Zora remained, in her writing, closest to her roots. When she worked, she worked hard, sometimes retiring from her own party to work in the next room.

In May 1927, Zora secretly drove to St. Augustine and married Herbert Sheen, who was using his musical talents to finance his medical education. "For the first time since my mother's death," she said, "there was someone who felt really close and warm to me."

They were very much in love, but both wanted their careers more than anything and almost from the start, she suspected the marriage wouldn't work. "It was not just my contract with my publishers, it was that I had things clawing inside of me that must be said," Zora said. The union lasted just eight months—so short and so secret that some doubted a marriage had ever taken place.

No longer bound to a husband, Zora signed a contract with Mrs. Rufus Osgood Mason, a wealthy patron of African-American arts. For a small salary, plus a movie camera and a car, Zora agreed to return to the South and collect folklore. She would use the material for her first book, but it would remain the exclusive property of Mrs. Mason, known as Godmother to her protégés.

Mrs. Mason sponsored other black artists, writers, and musicians, holding them strictly accountable for the smallest extra expenses, including medicine and bus fares. Zora, who frugally washed her face with laundry soap, once wrote from the field, begging "Godmother darling" for a pair of shoes, her big toe having burst through her right shoe. To modern ears, the letters might sound groveling, but she had no other funds to live on, except what little she could earn sporadically. Evidence of her determination to be a writer is revealed in another letter to a friend, in which she stated, "I shall wrassle me up a future or die trying."

Returning to Florida in 1928, Zora explored the turpentine and lumber camps, collecting "lying tales" similar to the ones she told as a child. She gained the trust of suspicious workers and their families by telling some of her own tales and by saying she was a Jacksonville bootlegger's woman to explain her car and clothes. She encountered barroom fights and possessive women, and things did occasionally get dangerous, so much so that Zora began carrying a revolver in her purse.

In 1929, when the country was battered by the Depression, even Godmother wasn't immune, and Zora's financial assistance ended abruptly. She returned to Florida where she wrote and published *Mules and Men,* described by respected folklorist Alan Lomax as "the best single book on Negro folklore in the United States."

Her short story "The Guilded Six Bits," published in *Story* magazine, attracted the attention of the J. B. Lippincott Publishing Company, which asked if she was, by chance, working on a novel. She wasn't but said she was and proceeded to write *Jonah's Gourd Vine* in about three months, according to her autobiography. She was in such financial distress that she had to borrow $1.83 for postage to send the manuscript to Lippincott. The company wired its acceptance on the same day Zora was evicted from her home for not paying eighteen dollars in rent.

In spite of intermittent successes, she was nearly always without funds to live. Brief employment as the drama coach at Bethune-Cookman College in Daytona, and then with the Federal Theatre Project, enabled her to survive until she received the first of two Guggenheim grants to study hoodoo in New Orleans, Jamaica, and Haiti. The mysterious, sometimes frightening, rituals of the Caribbean resulted in a manuscript called *Tell My Horse* and in a violent intestinal illness which, to her mind, might have been the result of a curse brought on by her subjects.

Still, during this period, she was able to write *Their Eyes Were Watching God,* a novel published in 1937 after she had left the Caribbean. The classic would be considered her greatest work, a statement of pride in her womanhood and in her blackness.

Not unexpectedly, it was criticized by some white critics who didn't seem to understand the book, and by black ones, including writer Richard Wright, who claimed it encouraged the "minstrel image" of blacks. As author-historian Mary Helen Washington would write in 1979, ". . . she was a black woman whose entire career output was subjected to the judgment of critics, both black and white, who were all men."

Returning to Florida in 1938 and subsisting on the last of her second Guggenheim grants, Zora joined the Florida Federal Writers' Project, which provided her with the means to write while caring for several of her nieces.

Zora diligently searched for other employment, knowing a conservative Congress was threatening to cut funds for the Writers' Project. She received an honorary doctorate from Morgan State and was on the cover of *Saturday Review* while fulfilling brief engagements at North Carolina College and Paramount Studios. The one-thousand-dollar Anisfield-Wolf Award she received at that time was especially welcome.

Just before leaving the Florida Federal Writers' Project, Zora married Albert Price, twenty-five years her junior. In less than a year, they were divorced, amidst bitter allegations from both sides, most notable being his claims of fearing for his life due to her use of black magic.

Zora moved to Daytona, living on a twenty-year-old houseboat. She rented a permanent berth for it, crammed it with books and papers, and proceeded to enjoy five of the happiest years of her life. She had it all: Florida, solitude, no segregation, sunshine, warmth. Crowning her joy was receiving the Howard University Distinguished Alumni Award.

When lack of money made a move necessary, Zora tried New York again, landing some odd jobs and a new publisher suggested by fellow Florida author Marjorie K. Rawlings. With a new book under way and several small sales, Zora's life appeared to be on the upswing until 1948, when she was astonished to be arrested, accused of molestation by a disturbed ten-year-old boy. The child's mother quickly dropped the charges when it was proven Zora was out of the country when the incident was alleged to have happened and it was further shown that Zora had told the resentful mother her unstable boy needed psychological help prior to when the charges were made. The painful incident would have ended there, but a black court employee leaked the story to a black Baltimore newspaper, the *Afro-American*.

Zora, devastated by sensational press coverage, wrote, "My country has failed me utterly. My race has seen fit to destroy me without reason, and with the vilest tools conceived of by man so far. . . . All that I have ever tried to do has proved useless. All that I have believed in has failed me. I have resolved to die."

She did not die. After a brief depression, she returned to the solace and warmth of Florida where she recovered enough to write again. Perpetually lacking funds, she was forced to pawn her typewriter, accept welfare, and do occasional substitute teaching. She rented the one-room cabin where she had written *Mules and Men* twenty years earlier and contentedly worked in her garden, writing constantly but with little success.

She started a new book, *Herod the Great.* Her enthusiasm returned, and then turned into overenthusiasm and obsession, so convinced was she that it would be her crowning achievement. She kept working on the giant book although her health began failing and she was forced to move from the cabin. With pride, she accepted an award at the Bethune-Cookman College commencement and then was compelled to take a job as librarian at Patrick Air Force Base, earning $1.88 per hour. To the annoyance of other workers and her superiors, she claimed she was the "best educated, most cultivated employee" there, and she might have been, but she was fired in less than a year.

When she was invited to write for a black weekly newspaper in Fort Pierce, she accepted, moving there and doing some substitute teaching at a segregated school nearby, along with the newspaper work. Overweight and in deteriorating health, Zora found concentration difficult after a stroke in 1959 and soon was unable to care for herself and, more important to her, unable to write. She was obliged to enter the St. Lucie welfare home, where, proud to the end, she refused help from her family. She died on January 28, 1960.

Donations paid for her funeral, which was attended by over one hundred people, black and white. She was buried in the Garden of Heavenly Rest in a grave unmarked for thirty years, until writer Alice Walker searched it out, had a gravestone installed, and, along with other writers, started a renaissance of interest in and study of Zora's work. It was here that Walker inscribed the moniker "Genius of the South" for Zora in 1973.

In his eulogy, the minister said, "They said she couldn't become a writer recognized by the world. But she did it. The Miami paper said she died poor. But she died rich. She did something."

In her autobiography, Zora had already said it better. "I have been in Sorrow's kitchen and licked out all the pots. Then I have stood on the peaky mountains wrappen in rainbows, with a harp and a sword in my hands."

HELEN HUNT WEST

1892–1964

LAWYER, JOURNALIST, FEMINIST

Describing her 1917 lobbying efforts on behalf of the federal women's suffrage amendment, young Helen Hunt, on vacation from her job with the *Florida Times-Union,* wrote:

> *I had believed if women went to Congress in a dignified way, and in a business-like manner put their case before that body of law-makers, they would be received in the same spirit and that in consideration of the fact that they represented a rather large proportion of the country's population, their question would receive serious attention. I had quite a shock coming to me. To say that I found a humorous side to lobbying would be expressing it mildly. I found a ludicrous side. While I met many able and intelligent men I was appalled and chagrined to find that many had not let the weight of their positions weigh very heavily on their shoulders.*

She went on to say, "The very first day, one Representative told me that women were too easily influenced by men, that a woman would always be more or less influenced by 'the persuasion of a good-looking man.' His final contradictory remark was, 'If you people want to gain votes tell them to send all of you young girls to lobby!'" Another representative unceremoniously told her to "go home and get married."

Helen Hunt's grandfather was Representative S. F. Grove of Georgia. Her great-grandfather was Representative Fred Hunter. Her cousin was Carl Vinson, a 1917 representative from Georgia. Being on a first-name basis with nearly the whole of the Florida and Georgia legislative contingents, she almost certainly made more of an impression in the corridors of the Senate and House office buildings than the average lobbyist. Certainly when Representative Vinson, whose sister was her childhood playmate, chastised her, saying he thought pickets were unwomanly, she reminded him that his sister Mabel was at that very moment standing on a street corner begging funds for Red Cross World War I relief work. Was it more bold to stand silently holding a flag, asking for consideration of an injustice, as she was doing, than to beg for dimes for the Red Cross, as his sister was, she asked cousin Carl. It was different, he said. She felt certain, though, that he began to see a "new light about that suffrage amendment."

Described in one newspaper account as having "a ready wit . . . a pair of very large dark eyes, a dimple in her chin, curly hair and not a single R in her vocabulary," Helen Hunt enjoyed her feminine prerogatives but at the same time could not be distracted from more serious issues. In view of the concerns relating to World War I, it seemed preposterous to her that women had to picket for their rights in the "land of the free and the home of the brave."

"Women are being called on to do their bit in this war crisis," she said. "They have always come to the front in every emergency. They are now asked to make a fight for a democracy in which they are not included. . . . Democracy is very near to our hearts; it has been for many years; like the men of the nation we are determined to fight for it—even if our fight means only taking a stand, only holding a flag."

She was determined to help right the wrongs of her own country, just as the men of the country were fighting to right the wrongs of other nations.

Helen Hunt was born on February 10, 1892, in Oakland, Florida, a village on the outskirts of Orlando. Her parents were Aaron Lancaster Hunt and Lillian Grove, mostly of English and American Quaker ancestry. Helen and her only sibling, her sister Clyde, were encouraged, especially by their mother, to pursue careers if that was what they wanted. "If a woman applies herself," Lillian said, "and is truly serious about a professional career, she should be successful."

It was not the usual path for young women in the early 1900s, but Helen chose to follow it. She attended Stetson Academy and then went on to the Florida State College for Women, now Florida State University, completing her classes in 1908, but not receiving her predated diploma until 1933 due to a dispute with some professors over completion of required course work.

After working for a year as assistant principal at Tarpon Springs High School, she joined the staff of the *St. Augustine Record* in 1911, remaining until 1913, when she began what would be a long, amicable employment on the editorial staff of the *Florida Times-Union* in Jacksonville. Writing mostly society columns, and then serving as society editor, Helen was ever mindful of her mother's advice to apply herself. Although employed full-time, she managed to study law in her off hours and was among the first women admitted to the Florida bar in 1917. "On my way to the exam, I felt I was carrying the weight of all the women of the world on my shoulders," she said. "I just knew if I didn't make the grade, the headlines would read, 'Woman Fails.' " Her grades were among the highest in the class.

As a child in Orange County, she had always been inexplicably attracted to the law. She received nothing but encouragement, she said, from her family members, who were mostly doctors and engineers. Setting up her law office in the Law Exchange Building in Jacksonville, she continued her career in journalism and began working hard for passage of the suffrage amendment.

Determined to make a contribution during World War I, she organized and became president of the Florida National Honor Guard, a group of four hundred Jacksonville women engaged in war relief work.

It was also in 1917 that Alice Paul, the Quaker lawyer and militant suffragist who had apprenticed in the British suffrage movement, spoke in Jacksonville, exerting a powerful influence on Helen. Shortly afterward, she joined the National Woman's Party (NWP), assuming the duties of chairman of the Florida NWP. At Alice Paul's suggestion, she undertook the difficult task of securing the signatures of thirty-eight representatives and seventeen senators on a petition for suffrage.

Representing the NWP, she was honored to receive the "prison special," a railroad car chartered to tour the nation by twenty-six women who had served prison sentences for demonstrating for suffrage. The women, wearing prison garb, made a sobering and lasting impression as they related the brutal treatment they suffered for demanding their rights.

Helen was one of the best-known suffrage workers in Florida when she decided to go to the capital and "see for myself just what was going on." What was going on was not encouraging.

President Woodrow Wilson had been vehemently opposed to the Nineteenth, or Anthony, Amendment, which would give women the vote. In addition, the city of Washington had been tense ever since a 1913 suffrage parade when suffragists had endured scathing comments that turned to contempt, and then violence. Newspapers generally had refused to print anything favorable to the women's movement, giving front-page coverage instead to the picket lines, complete with picture spreads ridiculing them. In dire need of favorable publicity, the women came up with a plan.

"We worded our picketing banners most carefully," Helen related afterward. "When news photographers would rush up to take a picture of 'those horrible pickets,' we made certain that the printed message on the banners would be in clear view. In that way we made every front page in the nation."

The messages were reasoned and intelligent. Helen's own banner proclaimed, "Governments derive their just powers from the consent of the governed."

Another prominent one said, "We will fight for the things we hold nearest our hearts . . . for democracy; for the right of those who submit to authority to have a voice in their own government." They were Wilson's own words, words spoken concerning foreign nations but glaringly appropriate to this domestic problem. As he passed the picket line, he stopped, read them, and passed on.

The publicity was having an effect; the tide of public opinion was turning into sympathy for the women. Before long, President Wilson joined the ever increasing numbers of lawmakers whose sympathies were with the women, and he asked Congress to pass the Anthony Amendment. They did so on August 26, 1920. Helen was the first woman to register to vote in Duval County in 1920.

She often stated that even tough men were not immune to flattery. According to her sister, who exchanged her own dreams of a legal career for life as a housewife, Helen was never one to disregard the power of her feminine wiles. One man she found enormously appealing was Byron McGonigal West, city editor at the *Florida Times-Union* in 1927. Tall, handsome, slender West had caught the eye of Helen and another woman working in the city room. Indeed, the other woman appeared to be the favored one until Helen took a trip to France. When she returned with a new bobbed hairstyle and a stunning Paris wardrobe, West's fate was sealed. Their wedding took place soon after, one day late for Valentine's Day on February 15, 1927.

With the passage of the Anthony Amendment, other women's organizations thought their battle was over, but believing that suffrage was only a first step to women's total equality, the National Woman's Party announced new goals; among them was working for passage of an Equal Rights Amendment.

In a speech, Helen said, "The proposed Equal Rights Amendment to the Constitution is one of those very simple things that has been made to appear complicated. It seeks not to make men and women equal—but only to make the law equal for men and women and, after all, that is democracy."

By 1923 the NWP was deserted by the Women's Division of the U.S. Department of Labor and the League of Women Voters, both of which promoted protective legislation for women workers. The NWP opposed such laws, favoring absolute equality in "the police force, in the shops and factory, in the schools, in the home." The party, whose numbers had shrunk after passage of the Nineteenth Amendment, was left with the enormous and unenviable challenge of raising the consciousness of legislators and women.

Helen Hunt West began making impassioned speeches before women's clubs. In 1935 she spoke to the Florida Federation of Women's Clubs, saying:

> *Women who are smug in their contentment in comfortable homes with husbands, brothers, and sons, of unreproachable character who minister to their every need, seldom pause to think that their own daughters and granddaughters have to look to an entirely different set of men for justice. . . . The only measure of security comes through the fundamental law of the land and that is the reason women need an Equal Rights Amendment to the Constitution of the United States. By the accident of birth we are women and we are dissatisfied with our inheritance of injustice and inequality. By the same accident of birth our brothers are men and they have inherited both. All we ask is the right to share that inheritance.*

As a lawyer with a growing practice, Helen felt obligated to familiarize women with discrepancies in laws where women were concerned. For instance, most legal papers women signed were worthless. Husbands could sue for their losses if their wives were injured, while wives could not if the situation was reversed. Fathers were not held accountable for

illegitimate children while women were in every way, including financially. Protective labor laws especially rankled her, believing as she did
that they were meant simply to deny women opportunity in industry.
What about housewives, she asked:

> ... *women whose hours in the home cover a period of twenty-four*
> *hours a day and include not only the dishwashing, cooking, sewing,*
> *scrubbing, garden work and thousands of nerve-trying and back-*
> *breaking tasks of the homes, but the training of little minds. . . .*
> *Those women . . . are seldom the subject of legislation. But let one*
> *of those mothers cross their threshold on unlimited working hours*
> *and set foot into a man-made world to earn a living for herself*
> *and her brood—she is immediately the target for protective legisla-*
> *tion—of laws enacted to limit her hours and her wages for her own*
> *good, while those of her male competitor are left subject to his own*
> *bargainings. He is then free to underbid her and get the job.*

In her concern for less fortunate women, she was instrumental in
founding the Panhellenic League in Jacksonville, an organization of
sorority sisters that sponsored scholarships for deserving young women
who wanted to attend college but couldn't afford it. Sorority sisters
were scarce in those days, but Helen doggedly persisted in her search
and rounded up twenty to attend the first meeting. She was elected the
League's first president.

In a convergence of her journalistic skills and her feminist sentiments, Helen functioned as editor of the *Southern Club Woman*. In a
1929 article, after watching a legislative session in Tallahassee, she
reported, "Some people may prefer vaudeville, the zoo or other forms of
amusement, but for me, I will take the legislature, and I think they were
right when they tried to pass that anti-monkey law. Everybody believes
in self-protection."

Helen was a Democrat and one of her greatest contributions to the Democratic party, and indeed to all Florida politics, was her 1935 work in piloting through the Florida legislature the "50-50" bill, which gave women equal representation with men on all committees of political parties in the state. Not unexpectedly, there were some opposition and some legislative "dirty tricks," inspiring her to begin a letter-writing campaign and visits to influential committee chairmen, one of whom made the unfortunate recommendation that she should "vamp" the chairman of the rules committee. In the end, the bill passed without anyone being vamped, opening up twenty-eight hundred party jobs to Florida women. Countering the general euphoria, one Democratic committeewoman said, "Don't expect too much, for the men will still try to get the most easily manipulated of our sex on to the committees."

While maintaining a home and office in Jacksonville, the Wests moved to Washington, D.C., in 1934. Byron was a syndicated columnist and a speechwriter for Washington politicians. He also did public relations work for several national organizations and traveled with Helen most of the time on her speaking tours as congressional and legislative chairman of the NWP. They, along with Helen's secretary, lived in a house on Constitution Avenue. In 1934 Helen gained admittance to practice before the Supreme Court, an outstanding honor.

From 1937 to 1940, she served as editor of the NWP's national magazine, *Equal Rights,* which provided favorable information on women's issues to newspapers and radio stations. During this period, she also spent much time on the thankless task of lobbying the U.S. Senate and House to inform lawmakers about the need for an equal rights amendment.

Speaking before the resolutions committee of the 1940 Republican National Convention, Helen urged the adoption of an equal rights plank. "The story of chivalry is beautifully idealistic," she said. "Most of us are accorded chivalry among our own menfolks but in the councils of the state, the councils of the country, the courts of the land and the associations of the nations, give us justice and we will take our chances on chivalry." The Republicans elected to support the ERA.

She also spoke to the resolutions committee at the Democratic National Convention, but the Democrats did not adopt the resolution until 1944, reportedly due to the resistance and influence of Eleanor Roosevelt.

On the other hand, not all was hard work during the Wests' stay in Washington. They enjoyed being acquainted with many famous people, including the actress Mary Pickford, Amelia Earhart, Pearl Buck, hostess Perle Mesta, and England's Lady Astor.

In 1940, when President Franklin Roosevelt was nominated by the Democrats to run for a third term, Helen accepted the chairmanship of the Woman's Division of the Anti-Third Term Democrats, saying, "It is inconsistent for anyone to take the position that a third term is wrong for all other presidents, but right for Mr. Roosevelt." She could not conscientiously vote for a third term for anyone, convinced as she was that the no-third-term tradition was one of the greatest safeguards our government has. "One step toward perpetuating any man in the office of president of the United States is one step too many on the road to dictatorship," she said.

She had, by that time, become disenchanted with the Democratic party, accusing FDR of disappointing women. She switched to the Republican party in 1940.

After the suspension of publication of *Equal Rights* in 1940, she was able to devote more time to her law practice but continued serving as second vice-chairman of the NWP from 1949 to 1956, while Byron resumed working on political campaigns and public relations.

Although she lost in her own 1942 run for Congress, she was gratified by the large numbers of men who were actively involved in promoting her candidacy.

A more profound loss came on April 3, 1952, when Byron suffered an acute coronary thrombosis and died.

As she had done all her life, Helen remained active in all her organizations, surviving and rebounding through her work. She was a member of the American Bar Association, the Florida Bar Association, the National Association of Women Lawyers, the National Federation of Business and Professional Women's Clubs, and the Junior Leagues of America. She served on the board of directors of the Elizabeth Edgar Home for Working Girls in Jacksonville and frequently appeared on panels, speaking in favor of equal pay for women.

Helen died after a brief illness on January 26, 1964, and was buried next to Byron in Evergreen Cemetery in Jacksonville. She willed her extensive library, mostly books about music and poetry, to Jacksonville University.

Although her name has faded from the general public's memory and the Equal Rights Amendment has not yet become reality, the many results of her determined efforts promoting equality for women are enduring monuments to the life of Helen Hunt West.

MARJORIE KINNAN RAWLINGS

1896–1953

PULITZER PRIZE WINNER AT CROSS CREEK

Fireflies flickered as the last game of hide-and-seek ended. Softly glowing gaslights along the neighborhood street signaled the close of a long summer day. On the stone steps of the church, little Marjorie Kinnan waited, immensely satisfied to have her playmates gather around her while one ran up and down the street calling, "Come on, everybody! Marjorie's going to tell stories!"

For as long as Marjorie could remember, two things she knew were true. One, she had a flair for making up stories. The other, she loved things in nature.

She was a child who noted the patterns of sunlight through the trees, the smells of the sea and its creatures when she vacationed with her family in Maine, the colors of new fall apples, and the taste of just-picked ears of corn when she visited her grandmother's farm.

In first grade, she relished the teacher's compliments for her poem "The Bluebirds." At age eleven, her story on the children's pages of the *Washington Post* earned the grand sum of two dollars. Other prizes and awards followed, strengthening her seemingly inborn destiny to be a writer, a destiny she never questioned, not even when she was spinning tales on the Baptist church steps.

Marjorie Kinnan was born in Washington, D.C., on August 8, 1896. Her father, Arthur Kinnan, a lawyer in the U.S. Patent Office, also owned a dairy farm that served as the family retreat. His pretty, intelligent baby daughter delighted him. "She is the joy of my life," he wrote. "I never knew I had so much love in my heart."

Marjorie Kinnan Rawlings   Photo by Erich Hartmann, Department of Special Collections, Smathers Libraries, University of Florida

Marjorie's mother, Ida Thaphagen, a supporter of women's suffrage and a former high school teacher, was a loving disciplinarian who, while insisting Marjorie dress and act like a lady, nevertheless, encouraged her to read and use her intelligence to prepare for a useful life.

She was four years old when her brother Artie was born. He was "her baby," she announced, and aside from occasional sibling bickering, the affection between them was obvious, her maternal feelings for him enduring for the rest of their lives.

She lived an idyllic life with her loving family in peaceful times. In the shadow of the nation's capital, influenced by politically minded parents, Marjorie and Artie were more knowledgeable than most children about the exciting events of the times. Automobiles and radios were becoming commonplace, the North and South Poles were being explored, and Teddy Roosevelt and his family were entertaining the nation with their antics.

Marjorie was assistant editor of her high school paper when the first tragedy in her life occurred. In 1913 her father suffered a kidney infection and died.

Influenced partly by his close relationship with Wisconsin's Senator Bob La Follette and impressed by the university's academic standards, Arthur had planned for his children to attend the University of Wisconsin. Ida had grown up in Michigan, so she was partial to the Great Lakes area and determined to carry out her husband's wishes. She arranged for the family to move to Madison, where Marjorie enrolled as an English major, with Artie following later.

After holding several positions on the staff of the school yearbook, Marjorie was selected to be an associate editor of the *Wisconsin Literary Magazine,* known as the *Lit.* She and fellow editor Charles Rawlings necessarily spent much time together. They fell in love, planning their marriage and their futures together as the war in Europe escalated.

When many male students at the university began enlisting, the mood on campus grew progressively gloomier, especially after reports of deaths and injuries started coming back. During their senior year, Chuck tried for a commission in the Army but failed, and after their graduation, he reported to Long Island for basic training as a buck private, much to his displeasure.

Marjorie planned to launch her writing career in New York City. With a briefcase stuffed with stories and poems, and sixty dollars from her mother in her purse, she traveled to New York, found a six-dollar-a-week room with kitchen privileges and began looking for a job. It was a fruitless, discouraging search for a lonely young woman. Her spirits plunged when she discovered her purse with the sixty dollars gone, stolen. Still, she had her briefcase with the papers inside, including a letter of introduction from one of her professors to an editor blocks away. Tearfully, she trudged to the editor's office where she received a sympathetic ear, if not a job. The editor wiped her tears and loaned her twenty dollars, telling her if she couldn't repay it, to pass the favor along to another beginner someday.

She did get a job, not the kind she wanted, but as a writer for the national headquarters of the YWCA. At the end of a year, she and Chuck were married.

After the war ended in 1919, the newlyweds moved briefly to Kentucky, and then to Chuck's hometown, Rochester, New York. Both were hired by the *Rochester Times-Union*, Chuck as a reporter, Marjorie as a feature writer. Along with human interest stories, Marjorie wrote poems under the title of "Songs of the Housewife," extolling the joys of washing pots and pans and scrubbing floors. The poems won her a following, but she was disappointed by the lack of success with her short stories.

In 1923 Marjorie's mother died unexpectedly at the age of fifty-two, probably from a stroke, leaving Marjorie a little money, which she put away for a rainy day.

She and Chuck decided to treat themselves to a boat trip to Florida, disembarking in Jacksonville, then touring by land the north-central interior of the state, far from the tourist meccas. Charmed by the remoteness, the natural beauty of the live oaks, and lakes, and the kindness of the native families, they impulsively made plans to move there, making good use of the money Ida had left Marjorie.

Included with their purchase of a rundown eight-room farmhouse on seventy-four acres of land were a four-room tenant house, a barn, thirty-three hundred orange trees, eight hundred pecan trees, and a number of other citrus trees. They hoped the spread would provide them with a living while they continued writing.

Almost before they were settled in the tiny village of Cross Creek, Marjorie, still fascinated with nature, began learning about the Florida plants and animals surrounding her new home. When they were buying their property, they met the local census taker, Zelma Cason, who introduced Marjorie to some of the reserved native people. Carefully copying their speech mannerisms on paper, she was intrigued with the deeply tanned, proudly self-reliant Crackers. The term "Cracker" was not pejorative, she learned, but another name for the rural white natives of Florida and Georgia. She filled notebooks with observations on them and on the native creatures, not excluding mosquitoes, snakes, and "no-see-ums." Before long, she sent a collection of "true sketches of the Cracker folk in the still pioneer heart of Florida," which she called "Cracker Chidlings," to *Scribner's Magazine*, where they were accepted.

Although the collection was received favorably, there were complaints from people involved in the tourist industry who protested that Marjorie should have glossed over the more unattractive traits of her neighbors. The editor of the *Ocala Evening Star* weighed in with his opinion that the sketches were "crude and unsympathetic" and "libel against the citizens of Florida." Marjorie's reply, in a long, scorching letter, proclaimed her admiration for the land and its people, defended the accuracy of her descriptions, and informed him that she had barely begun her writings.

She sent another story to Scribner's, and it was placed with Maxwell Perkins, the legendary editor who worked with Hemingway, Fitzgerald, and Thomas Wolfe. To her great delight, he recognized her talent and became her mentor, encouraging, suggesting, and helping her improve her skills.

Marjorie's unassuming, open neighborliness helped her make friends among the people of Cross Creek. She dressed like the local women in simple cotton housedresses and, in order to learn even more about them, she boarded with a family in the scrub country, learning to hunt and fish for food, make her own lye soap, scour floors with corn shuck brushes, and even how to make moonshine. At the end of the day, when her "family" fell into bed exhausted, she filled more notebooks with what she learned that day and would later reclaim in her writings. She became one of them to such a degree, she confessed to Perkins, "I am in some danger of losing all sophistication and perspective."

Her first book, *South Moon Under,* gave such accurate descriptions of fence building and making moonshine, they can be used as "how to" instructions. *South Moon Under* was chosen for a Book-of-the-Month Club selection.

While Marjorie's successes were accumulating, Chuck's were not, and he found the situation increasingly unbearable. In letters to close friends, she claimed she was more and more his scapegoat for all the failures of his work and their lives. They agreed to divorce.

After splurging on an adventurous trip on the St. John's River with a woman friend, she returned to Cross Creek, writing an article for *Scribner's Magazine* in which she said, "The creek was home. . . . my own shabby fields, weed-tangled, were newly dear."

In 1933 she won an O. Henry Award for the story "Gal Young Un," saw her divorce become final, and, with the encouragement of Perkins, started a novel about a boy. That book would become *The Yearling,* the signature work of her career. She also met Norton Baskin, who was four years her junior, looked much younger than she, and who would become increasingly important in her life.

While all this was going on, she alone had to oversee the household and groves. Often, when hired help failed to show up or became ill, she had to feed chickens, milk cows, and manage the grove workers. These tasks could daily consume six hours or more of her precious writing time, to say nothing of her energy. She strove for independence, to the extent of attempting to overcome her fear of snakes by going on a rattle-snake hunt with a herpetologist. By the end of the trip, she learned to manage her fear of dangerous snakes and even to tolerate a king snake inhabitant on her property; she eventually scratched his back at skin-shedding time.

When she finished work at six o'clock, she walked four miles. "Between punishing my thin brain and my fat body, I have nothing left by sunset but a swell set of cuss words," she told a friend.

To break up her punishing schedule, she fulfilled a contract to deliver two lectures at the University of Florida, where she captivated the audience, much as she had done on the church steps years before. "Don't let anyone talk of the delightful light life of the author," she told the students. "The moment you put down your title, your first line, you're in for a job of carpenter-work, of brick-laying, of roof-covering, of intricate plumbing."

The Yearling was published in 1938 to rave reviews, both from people in the publishing business and from scholars of literature and zoology. Letters from readers, many of them children, were especially gratifying to Marjorie. Named a Book-of-the-Month Club selection, *The Yearling* sold 240,000 copies in its first year, galvanizing the sale of movie rights and becoming a true classic. Awards and accolades poured in, culminating with her winning of the Pulitzer Prize over strong competition.

Life was exciting and fun again, with Norton Baskin making frequent trips to Cross Creek from the hotel he managed in St. Augustine. Through Perkins, she met more authors. She and Margaret Mitchell, author of *Gone with the Wind,* had much in common, including a loss of privacy due to curious tourists. Mitchell said they were people who "would just as soon have been viewing the Dionne quintuplets or a two-headed baby in a bottle of alcohol." To escape and be nearer to Norton, Marjorie bought a beach cottage in Crescent Beach for a hideaway.

One of the joys of success was being able to indulge her innate generosity. Even before she could afford it, she had pampered "baby" brother Artie, who was frequently in debt, some of it due to three unfortunate marriages. She was always available when neighbors or employees in her groves or household needed help. Now, she happily gave generous gifts at Christmas, paid hospital bills for her grove manager and her cook, and contributed substantial cash to Artie's business.

While excitement swirled about, Marjorie worked on short stories for an anthology and incubated the idea for a book about Cross Creek. She and Max Perkins agreed it would be a story of her own feelings about the place, its beauty, and her neighbors, an unusual book for the times. As work on it progressed, she sought his advice about whether any parts would be hurtful or libelous, since she used real names in most instances. "These people are my friends, and I would not be unkind for anything," she wrote. He reassured her, adding he thought it would be a fine book.

In 1941 Marjorie and Norton cemented their relationship in a brief marriage ceremony, and a few months later *Cross Creek* was published to immediate positive reviews. The book touched a chord with servicemen, recalling homey details and warm memories. It became her third Book-of-the-Month Club selection. Enthusiastic reader response to a chapter on food and recipes inspired her to write *Cross Creek Cookery*, a cookbook with recipes tested by her and her cook, Idella, interspersed among vignettes and nostalgia. It, too sold well.

By this time, World War II was changing everyone's lives by putting increasing numbers of people in uniform, plus causing gas and food rationing. To her dismay, Norton, overage for the draft, signed on as an ambulance driver. Patriotic Marjorie put a great deal of money into war bonds and devoted so much time to writing to servicemen, it interfered with her work on a new novel.

Worry about Norton's assignment to the India-Burma border understandably affected her frame of mind and contributed to her increasing reliance on alcohol. She and Norton had lived an unconventional lifestyle, he at his hotel in St. Augustine, she at Cross Creek, meeting frequently at Crescent Beach, but she needed his stabilizing influence. Admittedly moody and unable to do things in moderation, her hostile outbursts with household help, followed by tearful contrition, became more numerous.

After the war ended and Norton returned, Zelma Cason declared a war of her own, initiating a lawsuit against Marjorie because of what Zelma considered her slanderous portrayal in Cross Creek. Friends and neighbors rallied to Marjorie's side, confirming her descriptions of Zelma as a "profane, amusing, ageless spinster." Cross Creek natives sided with Marjorie and the court agreed, ruling against Zelma. Eventually, however, the Florida Supreme Court ruled in Zelma's favor when the charge was changed from libel to invasion of privacy. Zelma must have been disappointed with her award of just one dollar, but the mental cost to Marjorie was enormous. Including court costs and lawyer fees, the monetary bill was eighteen thousand dollars, but the toll on her health was considerable. Old difficulties with diverticulitis flared miserably, aggravated by alcohol and five and a half packs of unfiltered Lucky Strikes a day. All along, she felt she was fighting for a vital principle: ". . . the right of anyone to write of his or her own life, where that necessarily involves mention of other people, short, of course, of libel," she wrote in a letter to *Time* magazine.

Max Perkins's death in 1947 was another blow. She learned the news as she was beginning a new novel about a Michigan farm family. Friends had loaned her their farmhouse in upstate New York, and while she worked through her "unspeakable grief" with long walks through the woods, she became so captivated with her surroundings, she bought a small lakeside property. She intended to summer there, hoping the change would help her work, which was not going well in Florida.

Returning to Florida, she accepted an invitation to speak at then all-black Fisk University. Like many writers and artists, she scorned convention in social matters, including civil rights. Incensed by a *Jacksonville Times-Union* editorial favoring segregation, she wrote in the opinion page that she prayed for the editor's own liberation. "No man is free as long as another is enslaved," she said.

With a few days' work remaining on her latest novel, now entitled *The Sojourner*, Marjorie was alone at Cross Creek in 1952 when she awoke with terrific chest pain that persisted all night. Because there was no one to hear her call, she fully expected to die. When the maid found her the next day, Marjorie was whisked to a St. Augustine hospital, diagnosed as having suffered a heart attack, and kept for three weeks, lovingly supervised by Norton.

During her recovery at home, frustrated and depressed, she began drinking again.

Finally, after a decade's work, *The Sojourner* was published, to mixed reviews. Rejected by the Book-of-the-Month Club, it was accepted as a selection by the Literary Guild, but it didn't touch people the way her Florida writings did. She resisted the label of regional writer, but her Florida stories, in which the authenticity of her descriptions and the deep love and respect she felt for her neighbors came through, resonated with readers in a way her later works did not.

Although exhausted, she resumed working and started her usual extravagant Christmas preparations, sending gifts of Florida fruits to family and friends.

During a bridge game on December 12, 1953, she became ill but was convinced it was diverticulitis again. Norton rushed her to the hospital in St. Augustine, but by the following morning, she was dead from a ruptured cerebral aneurysm.

Norton wrote her simple epitaph: "Through her writings she endeared herself to the people of the world." It could be added: especially to the people of Florida.

Jacqueline Cochran

1906–1980
FLYING HIGH

When she died in 1980, she held more air speed, altitude, and distance records than any other pilot, male or female, in aviation history. Most of those records still stand. She was variously described as a woman who didn't mind bending the truth if she deemed it necessary, as an insufferable egotist with a personality like sandpaper, and as someone who came on like a human steamroller.

So poor as a child in the Florida Panhandle that she had no shoes until she was eight years old, she grew up to hobnob with presidents, European royalty, and movie stars. She was much ashamed of her childhood and her family's poverty, later claiming to be an orphan raised by a foster family, neither of which was true. Although she enthusiastically promoted the Women's Air Force Service Pilots (WASP) during World War II, years later, her testimony before a congressional committee helped torpedo the possibility of the first woman in space being an American.

Jacqueline Cochran, a study in contradictions, was born Bessie Lee Pittman, near Muscogee, Florida, in 1906. She quit school after the second grade to join her family working twelve-hour shifts for six cents an hour in the dusty textile mills of the western Panhandle. Occasionally, she was hired by pregnant women who worked in the textile mills to cook, wash diapers, mind other children, occasionally even to help bring babies into the world, all for ten cents a day.

For the rest of her life she would make sporadic attempts to become more literate. But as a child, there was little time for reading as she worked long, hard hours, giving most of her earnings to her mother, except for the few cents she saved for herself.

Jacqueline Cochran   Florida State Archives

When the mill's company store had a holiday display with a doll to be raffled off on Christmas Eve, Bessie, who had never owned anything beautiful, saved enough money to buy two raffle tickets. She dreamed of the doll for weeks and was ecstatic when she won. Her joy was short-lived though, shattered when her father made her give the doll to her niece, Willie Mae, who was a few years younger than Bessie. Though she mourned that loss into adulthood, grown-up Bessie provided financially for eighteen-year-old, down-and-out Willie Mae, in return for the doll that Willie Mae had kept all those years and that her aunt then refurbished and cherished for the rest of her life.

A strike at the mill motivated Bessie to enter a new phase in her young life. She started work at a beauty shop, at first cleaning and running errands. Then gradually, she learned the beauty business, even training to use a permanent wave machine.

Just fourteen years old when she married a young salesman named Robert Cochran, she gave birth to a son a few months later. The couple soon separated and she did not fight divorce proceedings instituted by her husband. When her parents volunteered to look after her baby boy, Bessie accepted their offer, grateful for the opportunity to return to the beauty business.

Before long, the restless young woman made up her mind to move to Montgomery, Alabama, to try her hand at the nursing profession. Although she lacked educational credentials, she liked helping people. But near the end of her training, Bessie suffered the heartbreaking news that Robert, her son who was four years old by then, had burned to death while playing with matches. Grief stricken, Bessie returned to her parents' home for her son's funeral; then deeply depressed, she stayed on until necessity forced her to earn some money.

Her depression began to lift when she found work in one of Pensacola's many beauty shops. Gradually, she even started to date and attend dances with pilots from the nearby naval air station, but she was not content. She made up her mind to try for a career in New York City's high-priced beauty salons.

She further decided it was time for a new beginning. She would no longer be Bessie Pittman Cochran from the Florida Panhandle. She would be Jacqueline Cochran; and with her new name, life seemed to turn a corner. Brazenly confident, she applied and was hired at Antoine's elegant salon in Saks Fifth Avenue. She did so well that Antoine sent Jackie to work that winter at his other salon in Miami Beach where doors opened that she never knew existed.

She made friends easily when she wanted to, and in the high society, yacht- and palm tree–atmosphere of Miami, Jackie wanted to, very much. She worked hard, rapidly built up a clientele of well-to-do women who invited her to join them at various social functions. At one of those cocktail parties at a swank Miami Beach hotel, she met Floyd Odlum, a multimillionaire businessman whose own marriage was unofficially over. Attracted to each other from the start, they married in 1936 shortly after his divorce. She had already begun flying as often as she could afford to, but his vast fortune enabled Jackie to fulfill two enduring dreams.

The dream of flying had long simmered in her mind, having lived for years near the Pensacola Naval Air Station, with the constant hum of airplanes, dates with aviators, and exposure to endless conversations about flying. Then after she had been treated to one thrilling ride in a friend's plane, she knew. She had to learn to fly.

With her second grade education, she could barely read or write, but she soloed after two days of flying lessons, took the test orally, signed the papers with an X, and became a licensed pilot in less than three weeks. It was 1932 and she was just getting started.

She flew every chance she got, accumulating flying hours, continuing with lessons, and in 1934 Jackie became a licensed commercial pilot.

Her second big dream was to form a company to sell her own brand of cosmetics, which for years she had been formulating and testing, simply because she believed women should always look their best and needed good cosmetics to do it. Floyd's backing enabled her to establish Jacqueline Cochran Cosmetics, which eventually grew to become a respected brand carried by major department stores.

Floyd encouraged Jackie to pursue both dreams. Convinced that a pilot's license would enable her to cover more business territory, he backed her with generous amounts of money. It was an excellent partnership.

Befitting Floyd's far-flung connections, they entertained lavishly at their 700-acre California ranch, where the guest lists included Walter Cronkite, Amelia Earhart, Billy Graham, Walt Disney, Bob Hope, and Presidents Eisenhower, Johnson, and Kennedy. Floyd lovingly financed Jackie's pursuit of flying records, glorying in her reflected successes. His backing, plus money from her cosmetic company, allowed her to compete frequently in national and international air races.

The 1935 Bendix Race, from Los Angeles to Cleveland, was a triumph for her and for another pilot who would become famous, Amelia Earhart. The triumph was not because either of them won, they didn't, but because their applications were at first denied due to their sex, then later accepted because of Jackie's persistence that the rules be changed. She did win first place in that race in 1938.

Jackie and Amelia became close friends, not rivals. They occasionally competed in the same race, but Jackie's specialty was speed, Amelia's generally was long distances. Jackie had truly broken the glass ceiling in aviation. If Amelia had not died so young, so dramatically, would Jackie be the more famous one? Many think so.

From 1934 to 1940, Jackie concentrated on setting records. She collected three speed records, set a new altitude record of 33,000 feet, and was a fourteen-time winner of the Clifford Burke Harmon Trophy as the world's outstanding woman flier. She was the first woman to make a totally blind instrument landing. She helped design the first oxygen mask and was the first pilot to fly above 20,000 feet to test it. She risked her life to fly many experimental flights to test gyro instruments and aircraft designs.

After she organized twenty-five women to fly for Great Britain in World War II, she was the first woman to fly a bomber across the Atlantic. She then directed the Women's Air Force Service Pilots, women who worked as test pilots, trained male pilots, and towed targets attached to a fifteen-hundred-foot cable for anti-aircraft gunners to practice firing at with live ammunition. Resented by male pilots, the WASPs would not receive their well-deserved veteran status until 1979. Jackie herself had even paid for their uniforms.

For her help in training over one thousand auxiliary pilots during the war, Jackie was awarded the Distinguished Service Medal. She gained the rank of lieutenant colonel in the Air Force Reserves, hobnobbed with generals, and visited both the European and Pacific theaters of war. The poor girl from the Panhandle was a guest at two presidential inaugurations.

Having pushed the boundaries for women pilots her whole life, she disappointed and angered most of them, particularly the thirteen women who had trained, passed all NASA's tests, and were passionate to fly into space. At age 56, too old to be an astronaut herself, Jackie sided with male pilots, astronauts, and politicians who chose to ignore the women's records and insisted women were unqualified to be astronauts. Her staunch support of John Glenn's damning testimony before a congressional committee was credited by many as finally ending any push for America to send the first woman into space. It was considered a shameful episode that demeaned a great aviator in countless women's eyes.

Jackie, the first woman to break the sound barrier at age forty-seven, wasn't finished. She went on to set eight speed records when she was over sixty years old, became a helicopter pilot at sixty-one. In 1992 she was inducted into the Florida Women's Hall of Fame.

Heart problems ended her flying career, but Floyd's death in 1979 ended her interest in life. She died on August 9, 1980, the greatest woman pilot in aviation history, according to her own autobiography.

Jacqueline Cochran, alias Bessie Pittman, was buried with her doll, the doll she won in the raffle as a child.

FRANCES LANGFORD

———— ◦•◦ ————

1913–2005

SWEETHEART OF WORLD WAR II

O riginally known as the "Florida Thrush," later she was called the "Sweetheart of World War II," and the "Sweetheart of the Fighting Fronts" for her selfless United Service Organization (USO) performances.

According to Bob Hope, with whom she toured, she was responsible for one of the biggest laughs he ever heard. On a far-flung South Pacific island, Hope had just introduced Frances Langford to the audience of hardened, war-weary Marines. She sang the first line of her most requested song, "I'm in the mood for love," when one of the homesick Marines stood and shouted, "You've come to the right place, honey!"

She shivered in head-to-toe woolies in Alaska and perspired in halter-tops in North Africa, but Frances would claim again and again until the end of her ninety-two years on earth, that entertaining the troops in World War II were the best years of her life.

A Florida native, Frances Newbern Langford was born in 1913 in Lakeland, a city near the center of the state. She grew up listening to and loving music. Her father, Vasco Langford, owned a pineapple grove in Martin County and worked in construction, but it was her mother, Ann, who believed in her daughter's talent and encouraged her musical dreams. A concert pianist, Ann played the piano while Frances listened, washing dishes and dreaming of a career as a soprano in the opera.

Throat surgery in her teenage years squashed that dream by lowering her voice to a register more suited to singing the blues than arias. With her mother's accompaniment and encouragement, Frances continued to sing every chance she got at high school assemblies, later for five

Frances Langford   Florida State Archives

dollars a week at a Tampa radio station, fifty miles away. Her big break came when Rudy Vallee, a major singer and band leader at that time, heard her sing and invited her to perform on his radio show. Following her first national radio broadcast, she signed a contract with a New York station and sixteen-year-old Frances was on her way to a long, glamorous career.

She enjoyed success in radio, then some small parts in films, but she rocketed to fame when she sang, "I'm in the Mood for Love" in an otherwise forgettable movie (*Every Night at Eight*, 1935). The sultry song would be with her for the rest of her career; her recording of it sold more than fifteen million records over the years.

In 1934 Frances married movie star Jon Hall. The marriage ended in divorce after seventeen years, but the two remained friends until his suicide in 1979.

When she filled in for Judy Garland on Bob Hope's radio program in May 1941, she began a long and very special association with the comedian. Her performances on his first USO tour that year at California's March Field were such a hit with the troops, she agreed to perform with him in overseas shows, the first woman to tour with the USO at a time when nurses were the only women permitted in combat zones.

Frances quickly learned to dodge bullets during aerial attacks and duck for cover in bombing raids. The Hope group performed closer to the front lines and to larger audiences than any other group. Famed WW II correspondent Ernie Pyle, who was with the troupe during two air raids, later testified as to the ferocity of the assaults the entertainers endured.

Frances was also one of the few entertainers willing to perform for the seriously wounded in the South Pacific, Italy, or wherever else men were hospitalized. She would claim the worst moment in her life happened in a Tunisia hospital when Hope asked her to sing for a wounded pilot, who was in bed, covered to his chin. She sang "Embraceable You," noting how the young man averted his eyes when she came to the line, "Above all, I want my arms about you," yet he never stopped smiling. Later, when she learned he had lost both arms, she was devastated.

She did cause a bit of an uproar by violating rules in the Pacific theater when she hitched a ride in a P38. Unexpectedly, the plane was forced into action during the flight, provoked to strafe a Japanese ship they encountered, but afterward things settled down quietly, and Frances was evidently forgiven.

She and her older brother, James, who was in the Coast Guard, always kept a lookout for each other during their tours overseas, but never did meet outside the states. Fortunately, they both survived the war and were reunited at home in Florida.

Along with the rest of Hope's troupe, Frances counted herself lucky when the plane that was carrying them all to Australia from Guam ran into mechanical problems and crashed into a river. The whole gang lost most of their clothes and several crates of spirits, but they were all safe.

General Dwight D. Eisenhower originally had reservations about women at the front, but he later graciously thanked Frances for her exemplary conduct.

There was something about seeing a pretty American girl who looked like the girls they left behind and who spoke like them that seemed to bring the weary soldiers home, for a little while at least. One soldier wrote to his family: "She will never know what she did for us ... For a few seconds, we were back in our natural surroundings and completely happy ..."

People found her wartime experiences so fascinating, the Hearst Syndicate hired her to write about them for a daily newspaper column entitled, "Purple Heart Diary." She later starred in a movie by the same name in which she played a character named Frances Langford.

Between USO tours, Frances continued making movies, mostly "B" movies, more noteworthy for her memorable vocal contributions than for her acting, but radio remained her special venue. She and Don

Ameche starred in the wildly popular radio comedy, "The Bickersons," and she headlined two radio shows of her own.

It was in the 1940s during her marriage to Hall that the five-foot-one-inch Florida native who loved to fish moved back home to Florida, to a beautiful spread in Jensen Beach. Once there, Frances donated a parcel of land to Martin County for a park, the beginning of what would in time amount to almost another career, this one in philanthropy.

Her marriage to Hall ended in 1953, and in 1955 she married Ralph Evinrude, chairman of the Outboard Marine Corporation, a *Fortune* 500 company founded by his family. A good match, Frances and Ralph shared an avid interest in boating and spent much of their time on their 118-foot yacht, *Chanticleer,* which they docked at their Jensen Beach estate. Together, they cruised to Mexico, Bermuda, the Dry Tortugas, and north to the waters of Canada's Georgian Bay, where they visited almost every year.

Together, the Evinrudes opened The Outrigger, a thatched-roof Polynesian restaurant and marina overlooking the Indian River. The restaurant became well known for its ambience, good food, and, if she was in the mood, in-person vocals by Frances Langford. It became hugely popular, both with the locals and with visiting celebrities like Bob Hope and Jackie Gleason. Now known as the Dolphin Bar and Shrimp House, its former owner is honored with a display of her photos in a room near its entrance.

Ralph Evinrude died in 1986, and in 1994 Frances married another outdoorsman, Harold C. Stuart, who had been Assistant Secretary of the Air Force under President Harry Truman. He was a lifelong supporter of wildlife conservation causes.

Frances loved nothing better than fishing from her boat. Even in her later years, when she needed the help of a cane to climb to the upper deck of the Chanticleer, her longtime captain said she would fish all day and sometimes all evening, breaking only for meals. To the Florida

Oceanographic Coastal Center in Martin County, she donated a collection of her preserved catches, including a huge blue-fin tuna, which she caught from the deck of the Chanticleer. The fish form an impressive display in the Frances Langford Visitor Center; and the annual Frances Langford Fishing Tournament is another reminder of her lifelong favorite pastime.

She continued to live in Jensen Beach and never ceased contributing to the community. She allowed the use of the Chanticleer for charitable functions, often serving as the gracious hostess. In order to serve her guests the very best, Frances did her own grocery shopping at the local Publix Supermarket, a market chain based in Lakeland, Florida, the town of her birth.

She also donated her time and money to the Florida Oceanographic Coastal Center, the Martin County Parks System, the Elliot Museum, and with the more than five million dollars donated to the Martin Memorial Hospital, she made it possible for a Heart Center to be opened, to provide vital services that formerly were only available long distances from home.

Never a mother herself, Frances and her foundation contributed to the Jensen Beach Little League, Safe Space, a skateboarding park, and Hibiscus House. Not forgetting the older folks, she donated millions to a new senior center. Her generosity benefited animals through the Humane Society and hurricane victims through the Red Cross.

Frances was inducted into the Florida Women's Hall of Fame in 2002, but she never sought name recognition for her good works. Fame as an entertainer was enough for her. Her name is attached in only a few instances, and then it was not her doing. She wanted to help good organizations, particularly some that lacked connections and were considered to be "under the radar."

Many people in Martin County were pleasantly shocked in 2007, when it was reported that in her lifetime (and to continue on through the foundation she created several years before her death), more than twenty-nine million dollars had already been donated to Martin County charitable organizations, an unmatched record of love for humankind from a Florida woman who never forgot her roots.

On July 11, 2005, Frances Langford died of congestive heart failure at age ninety-two at her home. Her ashes were scattered off the beach of her beloved Florida.

BIBLIOGRAPHY

General references

Douglas, Marjory Stoneman. *The Everglades: River of Grass*. Sarasota, FL: Pineapple Press, 1988.

——. *Florida: The Long Frontier*. New York: Harper & Row, 1967.

——. *Marjory Stoneman Douglas: Voice of the River*. Sarasota, FL: Pineapple Press, 1987.

Silverthorne, Elizabeth. *Marjorie Kinnan Rawlings: Sojourner at Cross Creek*. Woodstock, NY: Overlook Press, 1988.

Vance, Linda. *May Mann Jennings*. Gainesville, FL: University Press of Florida, 1985.

Webster's Dictionary of American Women. New York: Merriam-Webster, Inc., Smithmark Publishers, 1980.

Chapter 1: Malee Francis

Covington, James W. *The Seminoles of Florida*. Gainesville, FL: University Press of Florida, 1993.

Croffut, W. A., ed. *Fifty Years in Camp and Field: Diary of Major-General Ethan Allen Hitchcock, USA*. Freeport, NY: Books for Library Press. First published in 1909, reprinted in 1971.

Davis, T. Frederick. "Milly Francis and Duncan McKrimmon: An Authentic Florida Pocahontas." *Florida Historical Quarterly*, Vol. XXI, 1943.

Foreman, Grant, ed. *A Traveler in Indian Territory: The Journal of Ethan Allen Hitchcock*. Norman, OK: University of Oklahoma Press, 1930.

Georgia Journal. Milledgeville, GA. Nov. 3, 1818; Sept. 29, 1818; Oct. 13, 1818; Dec. 22, 1818.

Kersey, Harry A., Jr. "Private Societies and the Maintenance of Seminole Tribal Society, 1899–1957." *Florida Historical Quarterly*, Vol. LVI, No. 3, Jan. 1978.

Long, Ellen Call. *Florida Breezes: Florida New and Old*. Gainesville, FL: University of Florida Press, 1962. (Facsimile reproduction of 1883 edition.)

Mahon, John K. *History of the Second Seminole War, 1835-1842*. Gainesville, FL: University Press of Florida, 1992.

Peithman, Irvin M. *The Unconquered Seminole Indians*. St. Petersburg, FL: Great Outdoors Publishing Co., 1957.

Seminole Tribe of Florida. *History Where We Come From*. www.history.com. Accessed Feb. 20, 1999.

Wright, Leitch J. *Creeks and Seminoles*. Lincoln: University of Nebraska, 1986.

Chapter 2: Bertha Honoré Palmer

Grismer, Karl H. *The Story of Sarasota*. Sarasota, FL: M. E. Russell, 1946.

Lord, Walter. *The Good Years*. New York: Harper & Brothers, 1960.

Ross, Ishbel. *Silhouette in Diamonds*. New York: Harper & Brothers, 1960.

Swarthmore College Peace Collection, Jane Addams Papers. Series I, Microfilm, Reel 18.

Weatherford, Doris. *A History of Women in Tampa*. Commissioned by the Athena Society, Tampa, FL, 1991.

Chapter 3: Julia Tuttle

Allman, T. D. *Miami, City of the Future*. New York: Atlantic Monthly Press, 1987.

Blackman, E. V. *Miami and Dade County, Florida: Its Settlement, Progress and Achievement*. Washington, DC: Victor Rainholt, 1921.

Blackman, Lucy Worthington. *The Women of Florida*, Vol 2. Tallahassee: Southern Historical Publishing Associates, 1940.

Chandler, David Leon. *Henry Flagler: The Astonishing Life and Times of the Visionary Robber Baron Who Founded Florida*. New York: Macmillan, 1986.

Gannon, Michael. *Florida: A Short History*. Gainesville: University Press of Florida, 1993.

Gulliksen, Josie. "Julia Tuttle, A Miami Visionary." *Florida Living Magazine*. July, 1998.

Julia's Daughters. Narrative by Marie Anderson. Miami: Herstory of Florida, Inc., 1980.

Kleinburg, Howard. "Miami, The Way We Were." *Miami News*, 1985.

Miami Herald. Miami, FL. June 25, 1945; July 28, 1945; March 1, 1959; March 4, 1959; Dec. 13, 1965.

Miami News. Miami, FL. March 1, 1958.

Muir, Helen. *Miami, U.S.A.* New York: Henry Holt & Co., 1953.

Parks, Arva Moore. *Miami Memories: A New Pictorial Edition*. Published by Arva Parks in cooperation with Historical Association of Southern Florida, 1987.

Peters, Thelma. *Biscayne Country*. Miami, FL: Banyan Books, 1981.

Chapter 4: Mary McLeod Bethune

The American Negro Reference Book. Edited by John P. Davis. Englewood Cliffs, NJ: Prentice Hall, Inc., 1966.

Centennial History of Volusia County, Florida, 1854-1954. Edited by Ianthe Bond Hebel for the Volusia County Historical Commission, Deland, FL. Daytona, FL: College Publishing Co., 1955.

Chavez, Stella. "Top 50 Most Important Floridians of the 20th Century." *Ledger*, Lakeland, FL, May 18, 1999.

Flemming, Sheila Y. *The Life of Dr. Mary McLeod Bethune*. Daytona, FL: Bethune-Cookman College, 1999.

Halasa, Malu. *Mary McLeod Bethune*. New York: Chelsea House Publishers, 1989.

Hewitt, Nancy A. "Varieties of Women's Suffrage." *Forum, The Magazine of the Florida Humanities Council,* Tampa, FL, Winter 1995/1996.

Holt, Rackham. *Mary McLeod Bethune: A Biography.* New York: Doubleday, 1964.

Hughes, Langston. *The Langston Hughes Reader.* New York: George Braziller, Inc., 1958.

Tebeau, Charlton W. *A History of Florida.* Coral Gables, FL: University of Miami Press, 1980.

Warner, Carolyn. *Treasury of Women's Quotations.* Englewood Cliffs, NJ: Prentice Hall, Inc., 1992.

Chapter 5: Harriet Bedell

Covington, James W. *The Seminoles of Florida.* Gainesville: University Press of Florida, 1993.

Fort Myers News-Press. Fort Myers, FL. Feb. 20, 1952.

Hartley, William and Ellen. "White Sister of the Seminoles." *Coronet Magazine.* New York. August 1959.

———. *A Woman Set Apart.* New York: Dodd, Meade & Co., 1963.

Miami Herald, Miami, FL. Oct. 31, 1954; Aug. 22, 1959; Feb. 20, 1963.

Miami News, Miami, FL. Feb. 3, 1961.

Neill, Wilfred T. *Florida's Seminole Indians.* St. Petersburg, FL: Great Outdoors Association, 1956.

Orlando Sentinel, Orlando, FL. Jan. 24, 1965.

Tampa Tribune, Tampa, FL. Feb. 10, 1963.

Tebeau, Charlton W. *Florida's Last Frontier: The History of Collier County.* Coral Gables, FL: University of Miami Press, 1957.

Chapter 6: Eartha M. M. White

Bennett, Charles E. *Twelve on the River St. Johns.* Jacksonville: University of North Florida Press, 1989.

Crooks, James B. *Jacksonville after the Fire.* Gainesville: University Press of Florida, 1991.

Eartha M. M. White Collection. Thomas G. Carpenter Library. University of North Florida. Jacksonville, FL.

Florida Times-Union. Jacksonville, FL. Feb. 8, 1982; Sept. 20, 1987; May 7, 1988; Nov. 12, 1994.

Jones, Maxine D. "Without Compromise or Fear." *Florida Historical Quarterly,* Vol. LXXVII, No. 4, Spring 1999.

Ward, James Robertson. *Old Hickory's Town.* Jacksonville: Old Hickory's Town, Inc., 1985

Chapter 7: Dr. Anna Darrow

Fort Lauderdale Daily News. Fort Lauderdale, FL. April 5, 1955; Oct. 27, 1957.

Hanna, Alfred Jackson, and Kathryn Abbey Hanna. *Lake Okeechobee.* Indianapolis and New York: Bobbs-Merrill Company, 1948.

Journal of the Florida Medical Association. Tallahassee, FL. Vol. 55, No. 7, July 1968.

Lawrence, Will. *Cracker History of Okeechobee.* St. Petersburg, FL: Great Outdoor Publishing, 1964.

Miami Herald. Miami, FL. Oct. 28, 1948.

Ste. Claire, Dana. *Cracker: The Cracker Culture in Florida History.* Daytona, FL: The Museum of Arts and Sciences, 1998.

Tampa Tribune. Tampa, FL. July 17, 1955.

Women's Medical Journal. Harvard Medical School. Cambridge, MA. Nov. 1947, p. 48.

Chapter 8: Ruth Bryan Owen

Florida Biographical Dictionary. New York: Somerset Publishers, Inc., 1995.

Frank, Irene M., and David M. Brownstone. *Women's World.* New York: HarperCollins, 1995.

The Memoirs of Wm. J. Bryan by Himself and His Wife, Mary Baird Bryan. Philadelphia, Chicago, and Washington: The United Publishers of America, 1925.

Morris, Allen. "Florida's First Women Candidates." *Florida Historical Quarterly,* Vol. LXIII, No. 3, Jan. 1985.

Vickers, Sally. "Ruth Bryan Owen: Florida's First Congresswoman and Lifetime Activist." *Florida Historical Quarterly,* Vol. LXXVII, No. 4, Spring 1999.

Wilson, Charles Morrow. *The Commoner.* Garden City, NY: Doubleday & Co, 1970.

Chapter 9: Rose Sayetta Weiss

Anderson, Marie. *Julia's Daughters: Women in Dade's History.* Miami: E. A. Seeman Publishers, Inc., 1980.

Armbruster, Ann. *The Life and Times of Miami Beach.* New York: Alfred Knopf, Inc., 1995.

"Citizen's Summary, Miami Beach, FL." U.S. Dept. of Housing and Urban Development, April 11, 2000.

Folder on Rose Weiss from Sanford L. Ziff Jewish Museum of Florida. Miami Beach, FL.

Miami Beach Daily Sun. Miami Beach, FL. March 26, 1965.

Miami Beach Sun-Reporter. Miami Beach, FL. Aug. 8, 1974.

Miami Herald. Miami, FL. Aug. 8, 1974.

Miami News. Miami, FL. Aug. 8, 1974.

Redford, Polly. *Billion Dollar Sandbar: A Biography of Miami Beach.* New York: E. P. Dutton & Co., Inc., 1970.

The Reporter. Miami Beach, FL. May 15, 1957.

Weiss, Mrs. Eugene (Ruth). Phone conversations with author. Miami Beach, FL. April 10, 2000, and May 4, 2000.

Wittke, Carl. *We Who Build America*. Cleveland: The Press of Case Western Reserve University, revised edition 1967.

Chapter 10: Marjory Stoneman Douglas

Allman, T. D. *Miami, City of the Future*. New York: The Atlantic Monthly Press, 1987.

Burt, Al. *Becalmed in the Mullet Latitudes*. Melrose, FL: Miami Herald Publishing Co., 1983.

Graham, U.S. Senator Bob. Press release. Washington, D.C. May 14, 1998.

Jacksonville Times-Union. Jacksonville, FL. Nov. 15, 1998.

Marjory Stoneman Douglas High School Yearbook, Parkland, FL, 1991.

Miami Herald. Miami, FL. Oct. 5, 1997; May 14, 1998; May 15, 1998.

Sun Sentinel. Fort Lauderdale, FL. May 15, 1998.

Chapter 11: Zora Neale Hurston

African American Heritage of Florida. Edited by David R. Colburn and Jane L. Landers. Gainesville: University Press of Florida, 1995.

Bordelon, Pamela. *Go Gator and Muddy the Water*. New York: W. W. Norton & Co., 1999.

Glassman, Steve, and Kathryn Lee Seidel. *Zora in Florida*. Gainesville: University of Central Florida Press, 1991.

Hemenway, Robert E. *Zora Neale Hurston: A Literary Biography*. Urbana: The University of Illinois Press, 1980.

Hughes, Langston. *Langston Hughes Reader*. New York: George Braziller, Inc., 1958.

Hurston, Zora Neale. *Dust Tracks on a Road*. Originally published in 1942 by J. B. Lippincott, Inc., Harper Perennial Edition in 1996.

——. *I Love Myself When I Am Laughing*. Edited by Alice Walker. New York: The Feminist Press at City University of New York, 1979.

Lyons, Mary E. *Sorrow's Kitchen*. New York: Charles Scribners Sons, 1990.

McKissack, Patricia and Frederick. *Zora Neale Hurston: Writer and Storyteller*. Berkeley Heights, NJ: Enslow Publishers, Inc., 1992.

McMullen, Cary. "Top 50 Most Important Floridians of the 20th Century." *Ledger*, Lakeland, FL. June 18, 1999.

New York Times. New York, NY. May 20, 1999; Dec. 7, 1999.

Chapter 12: Helen Hunt West

Asheville Times. Asheville, NC. June 3, 1937.

Carver, Joan. "Women in Florida." *Journal of Politics*, Vol. 41, No. 3, Aug. 1979.

Jacksonville Metropolitan. Jacksonville, FL. Nov. 21, 1918.

Jacksonville Times-Union. Jacksonville, FL. Sept. 26, 1940; Aug. 20, 1949; March 4, 1950; Feb. 18, 1957; Jan. 27, 1964; Jan. 28, 1964; June 31, 1964.

Johnson, Kenneth R. "Florida Women Get the Vote." *Florida Historical Quarterly,* Vol. 48, No. 3, Jan. 1970.

McGovern, James R. "Helen Hunt West: Florida's Pioneer for ERA." *Florida Historical Quarterly,* Vol. LVII, No. 1, July 1978.

Schlesinger Library, The Radcliffe Institute for Advanced Study, Cambridge, MA, Box 1, Folder 1.

Sellers, Robin Jeanne. *Femina Perfecta: The Genesis of F.S.U.* Tallahassee: Florida State University, 1958.

Tampa Tribune. Tampa, FL. March 20, 1936.

Taylor, Elizabeth. "The Woman Suffrage Movement in Florida." *Florida Historical Quarterly,* Vol. XXXVI, No. 36, July 1957.

Vital Records Office. Jacksonville, FL. Phone conversation with author. Feb. 23, 2000.

Chapter 13: Marjorie Kinnan Rawlings

Bigelow, Gordon E., and Laura V. Monti, eds. *Selected Letters of Marjorie Kinnan Rawlings.* Gainesville: University Press of Florida, 1983.

Gannon, Michael. *Florida: A Short History.* Gainesville: University Press of Florida, 1993.

Glassman, Steve, and Kathryn Lee Seidel. *Zora in Florida.* Gainesville: University of Central Florida Press, 1991.

The Letters of Maxwell Perkins. Edited by John Hall Wheelock. New York: Charles Scribners Sons, 1979.

Parker, Idella. *Idella.* Gainesville: University Press of Florida, 1966.

Poems by Marjorie Kinnan Rawlings. Edited by Rodger Tarr. Gainesville: University Press of Florida, 1997.

Rawlings, Marjorie Kinnan. *Cross Creek.* New York: Macmillan, 1942.

Short Stories by Marjorie Kinnan Rawlings. Edited by Rodger Tarr. Gainesville: University Press of Florida, 1994.

Smiley, Nixon. *Florida, Land of Images.* Miami: E. A. Seeman Publishing, 1972.

Ste. Claire, Dana. *Cracker: The Cracker Culture in Florida History.* Daytona: The Museum of Arts and Sciences, 1998.

Tobias, Lucy B. "North Florida's Literary Legend." Marjorie Kinnan Rawlings Society. *Ocala Star Banner.* Ocala, FL. June 25, 1996.

Chapter 14: Jacqueline Cochran

Ackmann, Martha. *The Mercury Thirteen.* New York: Random House, 2003.

Cochran, Jaqueline, and Maryann Bucknum Brinley. *The Autobiography of the Greatest Woman Pilot in Aviation History.* New York: Bantam Books, 1987.

Getlin, Noel. "Eglin historian clarifies facts about aviation pioneer." Eglin Air Force Base, FL: Air Force Print News, 2009.

Rich, Doris. *Amelia Earhart: A Biography*. Washington, DC: Smithsonian Institute, 1989.

_____. *Jackie Cochran: Pilot in the Fastest Lane*. Gainesville, FL: University Press of Florida, 2007.

Yeager, General Chuck Y., and Leo Janos. *Yeager: An Autobiography*. New York: Bantam Books, 1985.

Chapter 15: Frances Langford

Allen, Diane Lacey. "Frances Langford Stuart." *The Ledger*. Lakeland, FL. Nov. 22, 1998.

Barrs, Jennifer. "Film Star, Singer, Bay Area Native Frances Langford Sang for Troops." *Tampa Tribune*. Tampa, FL. July 12, 2005.

Oldfather, Geoff. "Each of Us Owes a Debt of Gratitude to Frances Langford." Stuart, FL: TCPalm Florida's Treasure Coast, Dec. 16, 2007.

Time. February 28, 1944.

Exhibits at:

Elliott Museum. Stuart, FL.

Dolphin Bar and Shrimp House. Jensen Beach, FL.

Florida Oceanographic Coastal Center. Stuart, FL.

INDEX

County Operating Company,
    45, 46
"Cracker Chidlings," 124
Creek Indians, 2
Cross Creek, 120, 126, 127, 128
Cross Creek Cookery, 127

D

Darrow, Anna, 61
Darrow, Charles Roy, 60
Darrow, Dorothy, 62
Darrow, Dr. Anna, 60–68
Darrow, Richard, 61, 63
Daytona Educational and
    Industrial Training School
    for Negro Girls, 33
Daytona, Florida, 32, 33, 35
Denmark Caravan, 78
Distinguished Service Medal, 134
Douglas, Marjory Stoneman, x,
    91–100
Duke of Dade, 22, 23, 24
Dust Tracks on a Road, 103

E

Earhart, Amelia, 134
East Coast Railroad, 25, 62
Eatonville, Florida, 102, 105
Edwards, A.B., 15, 16
Eisenhower, General Dwight
    D., 139

"Embraceable You," 138
Equal Rights, 114, 115, 117,
    118, 119
equal rights amendment, 114, 117
Everglades, x, 45, 47, 77, 91,
    97, 99
Everglades National Park, 48, 49,
    96, 97, 100
*Everglades, River of Grass
    (The),* 97
Evinrude, Ralph, 140
Ewan, J.W., 22

F

"50-50" bill, 117
Fisher, Carl, 84, 87
Flagler, Henry, 23, 25, 26, 27, 28,
    32, 62
Florida Federal Writers'
    Project, 107
Florida National Honor
    Guard, 112
"Florida Thrush," 136
Florida Times-Union, 110,
    112, 114
Fort Dallas, 19, 23, 24
Fort Gadsden, 1, 3, 6
Fort Lauderdale, 67, 85, 88, 95
Fort St. Marks, 3, 5
Francis, Josiah. *See* Prophet
    Francis

Francis, Malee, x, 1–8